ABOUT THE AUTHOR

Frederic Will is currently Professor of Comparative Literature at the University of Massachusetts, Amherst. He has published a number of books of poetry, including *Mosaic, A Wedge of Words, Planets,* and a new book to be published shortly. *Intelligible Beauty in Aesthetic Thought,* and *Literature Inside Cut* are two other volumes that indicate Professor Will's wide scholarly interests. He has had Fulbright Grants to Greece and Germany, an ACLS fellowship, and a Bollingen Grant. At present he is concentrating, within scholarship, on Marxist literary criticism and the theory of translation. In connection with the latter he has, for some years, been editor and publisher of a poetry magazine, *Micromegas,* which features foreign national poetries in English translation.

HERONDAS

by Frederic Will

The chief aim of this book on Herondas is to present an up-to-date account of this Hellenistic poet's claim to lasting attention. The author has surveyed contemporary scholarship in an effort to learn what we know about Herondas today, as well as to analyze Herondas' texts closely in the light of that scholarship. In addition he has tried to discuss the development of scholarship on Herondas. This effort seems of particular importance for it enables us to see that Herondas is partly a product of a history of interpretations of him, and that we must start from those interpretations in any effort to get back to the original; that is, the study of an ancient poet is dependent on a tradition of studying him; scholarship is in that way a definite act of standing inside history. From this fact it follows that we cannot adopt a detached "scholarly" attitude toward even as seemingly un-contemporary a poet as Herondas. We must try to get back into the forces he embodies in his poetry and feel, from our historically conditioned standpoint, the pressure of those forces.

TWAYNE'S WORLD AUTHORS SERIES

A Survey of the World's Literature

Sylvia E. Bowman, Indiana University

GENERAL EDITOR

GREECE

Mary P. Gianos, Detroit Institute of Technology

EDITOR

Herondas

(*TWAS 227*)

TWAYNE'S WORLD AUTHORS SERIES (TWAS)

*The purpose of TWAS is to survey the major writers
—novelists, dramatists, historians, poets, philosophers,
and critics—of the nations of the world. Among the
national literatures covered are those of Australia,
Canada, China, Eastern Europe, France, Germany,
Greece, India, Italy, Japan, Latin America, the Neth-
erlands, New Zealand, Poland, Russia, Scandinavia,
Spain, and the African nations, as well as Hebrew,
Yiddish, and Latin Classical literatures. This survey is
complemented by Twayne's United States Authors
Series and English Authors Series.*

*The intent of each volume in these series is to present
a critical-analytical study of the works of the writer;
to include biographical and historical material that
may be necessary for understanding, appreciation,
and critical appraisal of the writer; and to present all
material in clear, concise English—but not to vitiate
the scholarly content of the work by doing so.*

Herondas

By FREDERIC WILL

University of Massachusetts

Twayne Publishers, Inc.   ::   New York

For Betty
es war möglich!

Preface

Herondas takes up few pages in histories of ancient Greek literature, even in histories of Hellenistic Greek literature, yet we
know how deceptive this index of value is. Scève, St. Évremond,
Chatterton, Morgenstern, and Leopardi get rather little attention
in histories of modern European literature, and yet they are unusually lively and seminal forces within their own traditions. To
realize this is to remember again how much mere hero-worship
goes into our establishment of a canon of the literary greats; to
what extent we simply admire the names proposed to us by our
national traditions; and to what extent we cling, for our own
security, to that ladder of familiar names. I. A. Richards, in his
Practical Criticism, long ago acquainted us with some of these
juvenile devices for closing ourselves to the whole complexity of
our literary tradition. We continue unashamedly in the old ruts.

Herondas is to some extent a victim of our literary prejudices.
He was (and is) a poet of limited range, writing in a limited genre
or subgenre (the mime) in a difficult allusive form of late ancient
Greek. This book will concern itself in part with the special difficulty of getting ourselves back into Herondas's language world.
Yet once we have found Herondas, as by now many have, we see
how lively and creative he was. We are in a position to value him.
The details of our evaluation will vary greatly according to our
personal tastes—he is not a poet for everyone, and perhaps not
a great poet for anyone; but we will see that he was a poet of
quality and high craft, and that he engages with our time. That
it is difficult for us to see this about him can in part be attributed
to his victimization by literary prejudice.

The tradition which suppresses Herondas reflects not only a
general trend of taste but an important bias within the literary
history, both of the text of Herondas and of the ancient world in
general. We can turn first to the historical questions. The present

text of Herondas was unknown until 1891, when papyrus containing eight of his mimes was discovered.[1] This lateness of discovery was disadvantageous for him. When it comes to the formation of literary traditions, the rule is first come first served, and Herondas came late, even in comparison to his Hellenistic co-writers. The oldest extant manuscripts of Theocritos go back to the thirteenth century: at that time copies of them were widely distributed throughout Italy. Similar histories apply to the cases of Apollonios Rhodios and Kallimakhos. The popularity of those two learned poets seems to have assured them a continuous, though limited, life throughout the Middle Ages.[2] By the time of the discovery of Herondas all the positions in the canon had been filled.

Within the literary history of antiquity the Hellenistic period had from the beginning received the least attention, and seemed the last candidate for canonization. The reasons for this prejudice are deep, and understanding it, even at our late moment of the Classical Tradition, might help us to understand some of our cultural motives more clearly. We need to pause briefly on the cultural history involved here, for it touches very directly on the strategy of clearing the ground for Herondas. A certain amount of preliminary spiritual archeology is necessary, before we can bring a man like Herondas into the light.

The notion that the fifth century in Athens was the center of gravity of ancient Greek culture only very gradually imposed itself. It was, for example, no part of the view of Hellenism which we find in the thinkers of the Middle Ages. From the end of antiquity until the birth of Humanism the heroic figures were epic writers—Homer and Virgil especially, and philosophers—Plato and especially Aristotle. Greek tragedy, for instance, was barely known. But not only tragedy. In *The Renaissance of the Twelfth Century*, Haskins shows how nearly exclusively the scholars of Greek in that period concerned themselves with "medicine, mathematics, philosophy, and theology." The problems facing those scholars were largely material; there was a serious shortage of texts. There were many other material factors at work. The land of Greece, with its gorgeous and coercive fifth-century remains, was almost totally unknown to the world beyond it. The general ignorance of the appearance or significance of a temple like the Parthenon is characteristic of the general ignorance of the fifth century in the entire Middle Ages.

The Renaissance sees the beginning of a very gradual shift in the center of cultural gravity; a shift toward the fifth century. The reasons for this shift are immensely complex—as complex in many ways as the entire growth of the Renaissance itself. Italy itself in the fifteenth century fostered a political situation which found some of its models in the democracy of fifth-century Athens. For pedagogical reasons the Greek of fifth-century Athens began to recommend itself; nowhere else could such a rich and supple language be found. (A seemingly small point which was actually very large, in an age which put great stress on humanistic education.) Finally—and this may have been the most widely influential cultural development—people began once more to go to Greece where, as we know, from the seventeenth century on travelers registered their impressions of monuments, the Parthenon, Bassae, Phigaleia, which represented fifth-century Greece at its plastic best.

From this point on the canonization of fifth-century Athens proceeded more efficiently.[3] The reasons sketched above accumulate new force around them. New reasons are added to them. One of the most significant is the shift in literary values. The worship of Aristotle is converted into a worship of ancient tragedy, which —in Jonson or Racine or Corneille—is taken to embody Aristotelian principles. Sophocles and Aeschylos take the stage, and though few men can read them, some can, while others can translate them or read them in translation. To this shift in literary values must be added an increasing attention to the democratic values of fifth-century Athens; to the peculiar sophistication reached by the Greek language at that time; and to the full-scale rediscovery of Greece itself, a rediscovery which seemed inevitably to direct its primary attention to Periclean Athens.

The canonization involved here grows deeply from literary prejudices and tends to confirm those same prejudices. The opposite of the same development was quite naturally taking place, with regard to other time sectors of the ancient Greek achievement. The Hellenistic period particularly fell loser to the gains of the fifth century. It is impossible here to do much more than state the culture-historical situation: that from the Renaissance to our day both classicists and men of culture in general have learned to look down on the achievements of the World Imperium which was created by Alexander and left to his successors. The sensational achievements of Hellenistic astronomy, mathematics, and medicine have, it is true, their pages in every history devoted to those matters. That place has been assured since the Renaissance, in which scholars were so generally ready to appreciate the Arabs' scientific achievements, and behind them, transmitted through them, those of the Greeks. But Hellenistic philosophy, politics, religion, sculpture, architecture, and literature have all been disparaged, or more often simply neglected. It is not the point whether such disparagement or neglect is justified. The only point is that factors were at work, in establishing this generalized judgment, which were products of cultural bias: of a bias against the image of the world of Alexander's successors.

Within the already off-center body of Hellenistic literature, as we often present it to ourselves in our day, the work of Herondas seems particularly off center, both because of its late arrival and because of its intrinsic character. There is only one reason to mention that character here in a preface; to extend my explanation of the relative neglect of Herondas and so to prepare his way to speak for himself.

Herondas is the least edifying of the unedifying Hellenistic poets: none of those writers wrote for a posterity which would turn its attention to the great human values, which would need to find, at the center of its literary canon, works which edified, works which reflected back the superego values with which posterity needs to maintain itself. (I think of a kind of criticism represented, at its best, by F. R. Leavis's *The Great Tradition*.) In fact, we find a very special relation adopted, by Callimachos, Theocritos, or Apollonios Rhodios, toward the cultures or ages which they imagined would follow them. They adopt, toward those coming ages, the pose of connoisseurs, of adepts of the highest verbal craft; they address themselves across the ages to the literary elite. When Callimachos writes that "a big book is a big evil," he means even more than he says; he means something intelligible only in the context of his whole body of work. He stresses his interest in careful workmanship, in precise expression, and in pure aesthetic values. Apollonios Rhodios, as an epic writer—author of the *Argonautica*—in one way, quantitatively, invited Callimachos's attack. However, a second look at his epic shows how far it is from the classical epic tradition. The *Argonautica* is a carefully chiseled, and indefinitely elaborated sequence of verbal embroideries on mythological material accessible (no doubt also intelligible) in Apollonios's day only to the very learned. Herondas shares much with both these contemporaries; not least his immaculate and self-conscious use of both language and literary devices. To this bond he adds his own specialty; a kind of aestheticism, joined to moral indifference, which puzzles and alienates many, and at best perhaps fascinates others who read him. Where that moral indifference turns toward a dabbling in the perverse, or even in the banally evil, Herondas tends to exceed the company of his own more purely aesthetic contemporaries—men to whom language became interesting to the degree that it became an ikon. Needless to say, Herondas also, at the same time, erects barriers between his text and later readers. (Who may well pull him off the shelf *in camera,* but will not put him on the reading list for their classes.)

ii

We have to clear the ground for a reading of the lesser known figures in our literary tradition, a tradition which belongs equally to each of us, and through the paths of which there are no privileged guides. In clearing this ground we learn a great deal of importance about ourselves as makers of canonical traditions, and, incidentally, as human beings thinking about and organizing their own past. This incidental discovery can be applied to many spheres of problems, for instance to those raised by the sociology of knowledge or the philosophy of history.

I mentioned three different respects in which a good reading of Herondas requires thinking our way past certain obstacles: we need to see past a prejudice against Hellenistic literature in general, a prejudice which is not active and omnipresent, but which simply spreads a light veil over the later achievements of the ancient Greeks—and which grows into a heavier veil over even later Greek literature, for instance over Lucian, Epictetus, or the Greek Fathers of the Church; we need to see past a sense of nonbelonging that pertains to Herondas because of the late discovery of his text—a sense that he is a new arrival on the literary scene; and finally we have to read our way past what seems amoral or immoral in Herondas's texts. None of these difficulties is vast; nor is the prize for surmounting them one of the great human literary experiences. It is a question, first of all, of going straight to where an author is, and finding out who he is. It is simultaneously a question of learning more about where our own peculiar prejudices lie.

The Herondas we find, on the other side of these prejudices, is the subject of this book. We find that he stands alone successfully. Two remarks should be made about the strategy used in bringing out the texts of Herondas here. I mean the strategies which surround, and I hope open out, the center of the book, the analysis of Herondas's mimes.

I open with a fairly long discussion of the "historical-cultural" background to Herondas's work. For such an author this kind of context-establishing is necessary. We know several reasons for the necessity. There is very little material evidence, from the immediate context of Herondas's life, with which to try to explain his life or the works that came out of his life. (Even if we think that works can be explained, or accounted for, in terms of life.) We know a probable birthplace (the island of Cos), a probable primary residence (Alexandria), and a probable *floruit* (the reign of Ptolemy Philadelphos). Beyond that we are on our own, left to the skill with which we can bring together the large knowledge we have of Alexandrian political and social history, with the precise and detailed knowledge we have of the vestigial remains of Herondas's writing. In this matter we can only go so far on our own, because the terms involved in the comparison are too widely separated.

We have to go into the ancient writer's historical-cultural past, where there is more abundant material, and—we find to our surprise, though we should have expected it—where there is material more relevant to understanding of the writer's work. Once again the lack of positive information about an ancient writer, or about the circumstances in which he lived, forces us to turn to sources of understanding which are actually among the most essential available to us in any literary inquiry, whether we have hard data or not. We are prevented from dwelling on any adventitiously material details, and we are encouraged to consider what is essential in the author's spiritual past. But it is not only a question of the essential. In fact we are face to face, at just this point, with a problem in literary explanation which is central to the whole undertaking of criticism. We face the question of what counts in the background, what is of account in making a literary production possible.

In modern criticism many attacks have been leveled against the cruder forms of accounting for an author's work in terms of his life. There is no longer much disagreement about the relevance of those attacks. Sartre's biography of Baudelaire, for example, helped us to see just what, in the material and social conditioning of an artist, can become viable and relevant in his work, and just how that material can become relevant. This kind of territory has been decisively won for criticism.

However, an author exists in a language, and in a language which has a history; and undoubtedly one of the freshest perspectives we can adopt, onto the significance of a writer, is to think of his work as something happening within the history of his own language. This kind of interest draws our attention to the *literarity* of literary texts, to that point at which, in them, "ordinary" language turns into literary language; but it also directs us to the question of the author's position within his tradition, in a most forceful and concrete way. We are led, in this way, not back into an idle exercise in linguistics but into a general concern with a writer's historically laden language, as it presents itself to him in any given moment. Historically laden means, also, culturally laden; for language is the main bearer of culture.

The strategy of placing Herondas within the far-reaching tradition which precedes him, in ancient Greece, is calculated to give some depth to the later discussions of his texts; for those texts were made out of a language which was in no sense invented by Herondas, which was in every sense appropriated by him, and played with by him, according to the rules his language allowed. (The contemporary French distinction between *langue* and *parole* applies exactly to the present distinction between public language and private use; see Roland Barthe's *Writing Degree Zero*.)[4] I have tried to open my first chapter with a cultural-literary-language picture of the Greek tradition available to Herondas when he came to write his mimes.

Drawing that kind of picture in language or—to change the metaphor—setting the stage in that way, involves a curiously difficult problem in perspective. I wrote here (briefly) about the epic, lyric, and dramatic genres which preceded Herondas's age, about the cultural environment which surrounded those genres, and about the way Herondas appropriated them. Yet this kind of setting the stage remains at best an outside job; an effort to say, from the outside of a particular historical tradition, and from a different perspective in human time, something about the way the particular tradition of ancient Greek literature presented itself to Herondas and was appropriated by him in his concrete moment. I am describing a deeper problem than that raised by determining the relativity of historical knowledge; the problem so thoroughly discussed, for instance, by Maurice Mandelbaum in his book *Historical Knowledge*. The problem in perspective is deeper. We are simply not inside the historical forces in which Herondas was; we are inside our own forces, which of course inevitably bear some of the weight of Herondas's forces. We are not entirely outside his tradition. We would not even be entirely outside the tradition of Druidic kenning literature or Siberian animal literature. But we cannot nearly stand where Herondas stood, or feel, in the network of forces which constitute earlier Greek culture, the totally present, undifferentiated, temporally immediate quality which Herondas felt. Anyone writing poetry in English today will confirm the peculiar and distinctive pressure exercised on him by the poetic tradition immediately relevant to him; he will agree that there is a certain foreshortening, a certain lack of distancing, to that tradition, which does not mark other traditions—say the tradition of developing knowledge in physics —with which he is less directly involved. We can imagine a parallel situation for a poet like Herondas. But we can go even beyond the parallel.

At the risk of overstating this point, which will of course be made when we come directly to Herondas's texts, we need to add that not even the Greek 'historical sense'—no matter to what phase of the Hellenic past it is applied—is like ours. We come to history, whether of literature, science, or politics, seasoned by the scientific, in many ways positivistic, attitudes of nineteenth-century historiography. Herondas had before him a tradition— Thucydides and even Herodotos—of brilliant exposition of human affairs, but very little tradition of exact data accumulation, objective analysis, or of that distanced stance between historical observer and historically observed, which blesses and threatens history writing with the possibilities of becoming a "science."

To make this point is to introduce the second strategy by which I have surrounded, and tried to open out, the texts of Herondas.

I have made special use of the opportunity provided, in this series of books, to devote attention to the effects and later resonances of the author in question. What might seem an unfertile topic, in view of the late discovery and relative obscurity of Herondas, is in fact a particularly fertile topic—once we decide to take scholarship seriously as a record of human experience. For Herondas's afterlife has, so far, been largely dependent on the scholars. A few translators have reached out to him, and even fewer poets.

This situation might seem an ominous threat to the success of a final chapter on the afterlife of Herondas's work, but in fact threat and apparent dearth can once again here be turned to advantage; as they were in the case of the dearth of contemporary explanatory material and social data, a dearth which forced attention back onto a broadly operative spiritual heritage. (An argument which must, however, be stopped short of the paradox that the less we know immediately around the text of an author the more we will be able to understand of him. We are talking here only of a certain kind of creative ignorance, not of a cult of ignorance.) In the present case, dearth can make us look closely at scholarship; and in so doing can make us rethink some old favorite prejudices.

One of those prejudices is that scholarship is a totally different activity from poetry or fiction. Another is that the history of scholarship itself is only of secondary, or derivative, interest.

If scholarship is as different from "creative work" as the cliché assumes, then the study of the scholarship about an ancient poet will be a futile study of a peculiarly arid relationship—between a scholarship and a poetry which are inherently unrelated to one another. If the history of scholarship is itself looked on as of derivative interest, then the study of the scholarship, about a particular poet, will be deprived of any inherent claim on our interest. But if scholarship can reach toward poetry, and if works of scholarship—say of the same poet—enjoy a creative relationship to one another, then a study of the significant scholarship on a significant poet should not be arid at all. If the last chapter of this book is arid the fault will be entirely mine, not inherent in the matter.

It will in fact appear there that the texts of Herondas are continuous with some of the texts about them; and that this continuity is eminently worth thinking through. The question of *continuity* here is of course difficult; and only through details will it be possible to earn a definition for the word in this context. The general point, however, involves a critical issue in literary epistemology, which can and should be addressed at its own level of generality, and preferably here in the preface, rather than in the closer and more bound discussion which follows.

Continuity between the text of an ancient poet and that of a twentieth-century scholar? Is it possible, in any but the most general sense? Is it a meaningful notion, not just part of cultural rhetoric?

We can test this question by a moment's reflection on four large and ambitious editions of Herondas: that of Nairn (1904); that of Headlam and Knox (1922); that of Otto Crusius (1926); and most recently that of Giulio Puccioni (1950). At first it seems that in these editions we encounter textual scholarship at its most mechanical and technical form. But this impression dispels itself at once, when we notice carefully what is taking place on even the most limited sector of these works, in the area of work in which they simply try to establish correct and reliable texts. Choices are revealing themselves there: choices of particular readings of unclear or fragmentary manuscripts; choices among the various orders in which those readings can be arranged; and, most important, suggested restorations of unclear or damaged passages of the manuscript texts. I restrict myself here to mentioning the basic work that goes on in the four books I listed. That basic work is in every sense already literary criticism, for it involves this kind of choice. I think we can speak, without falling into any kind of exaggeration, of such choice as a continuity between scholarship and the poetry it restores. And of course I am still speaking here of choice which is relatively a matter of training, competence, and skill; we aren't yet speaking of scholarship as the bearer forward, through ideas and embodied concepts, of the arcs of inspiration begun in ancient poems. We can discuss that level of continuity later, and will find some examples of it.

Among instances even of good editing, such as the four mentioned here, a creative interrelationship establishes itself which is part of that dialogue, within scholarship, which constitutes the whole body of scholarship as a response to its objects. Emendation answers to emendation and on the whole, though steps backward often intercept progress, we develop a more adequate equipment not only for understanding and interpretation but for encounter, and for maintenance of the past. When it comes to more explicitly critical and philosophical works, within the body of scholarship, it is still easier to see that those works create a living continuity among themselves.

The final chapter, then, will be largely devoted to the encounter of scholarship with Herondas. It will take up the character of that encounter, as it relates to Herondas himself, and as it forms a unity of its own.

iii

One more general matter remains to discuss, a matter of such wide interest that it seems almost too narrowing to say of it that it is properly prefatory stuff. It is, if anything, material for the preface to all prefaces, and while it may seem pompous to reach back that far, at this point, it is a job that needs doing.

I have discussed continuity enough to have made it into a key term of the present argument: continuity of Herondas with his own cultural heritage, of scholarship with Herondas, of different scholarly testimonies among each other. I want to think that speaking of continuity, in these ways, is not simply a facile way of describing what takes place in any cognitive act, in any act by which a knower establishes a bridge of meaning with another person or object. I hope I have made my point, that in all the instances involved here it is of central importance both that continuity is being maintained in language, in verbal art, and that it is in fact being maintained at all. It is certainly not in place here to unfold a philosophy of history around the present notions of literary tradition; but it is in place to see that the skeleton of very particular philosophical assumptions lies just under the surface of the arguments made earlier in this preface.

Onto those philosophical assumptions I want to build a final structure of continuity, that which binds us—first of all I mean me—to Herondas as an object of concern. I am thinking of that ground of continuity without which, of course, the other continuities in which I see Herondas embedded would be idle figments of perception. Is there, between me now and Herondas, the kind of continuity necessary to sustain the present book?

I ask this here because it forces itself on me, and because it belongs in the beginning; though there is some irregularity in asking about Herondas in this manner before he has actually been reached in discussion. A vicious circle is sketched here. How can we know, before we begin to study an author, whether he is worth studying? It seems that we need some guarantee, which is in fact missing. We cannot know that he is worth studying until we have finished studying him, yet in order to believe in him sufficiently to start studying him we must think that he is worth studying. Fortunately, existence, which puts the matter on a different level, intervenes at this point. It undercuts logic. Existence is a constant cutting through vicious circles, a risking oneself forward, testing the value of experience in the process of experience. Herondas became, becomes, for me one of those tests. But the test presents itself in an unfamiliar form. During part of this experiment I am faced with turbulence in my university; with strikes, boycotts, actions that raise for reconsideration the whole question of what a university is. (All of Newman's famous questions need to be rethought.) To some degree that turbulence is part of the general background for "thinking" man in our, or in any, time. The syllogism is often constructed against the noise of the siren. But I would be dishonest to myself if I ignored the special form this background assumes now, in my (in our) own reality. Students come to my door asking how I can consider it relevant to 'work on Herondas,' or to do something, anything, like that, "when our society is on trial in the streets." The question is hard, especially for a person who on the whole sympathizes with those questions and is painful at least to the extent that it makes me reconsider the whole purpose of my work. (It is hard enough to do the work, without having to reconsider it.) What can I say to my students and myself?

The continuity I take it on me to establish, between myself and Herondas, can of course not be guaranteed or validated from the outset; and so cannot be defended from its inception on any secure grounds. (In this, though, it is like all other continuities the critic might want to establish; even those between himself and the 'great writers,' Shakespeare or Goethe.) I think the insecurity of the available grounds forms precisely the point from which I must argue, in defending this establishment of a continuity which will embrace the other continuities discussed earlier. I affirm Herondas and he takes on his particular existence, for me, as a result of that affirmation. What could be more revolutionary, in essence, than this kind of free act of new creation, this kind of projecting a chance forward? (Especially at a time when revolution as happening, or chance, is being honored; as by Norman Mailer in *The Armies of the Night*.) But this is not enough of an answer either for the intelligent student at the office door or for the self-critic in my own mind. In fact, this is only enough to introduce one of the most difficult problems facing both the scholar and the political revolutionary. Why commit oneself to this particular *x* or *y*?

We can at least begin to amplify an answer which may be more satisfactory. There is in fact a kind of inner chancing involved in the type of commitment I am considering here, but the element of chance should not be taken as anything like pure happening. As we grow up through and into our own lives in language, and into the values language has in our own cultural world, we get a sense of what kinds of language correspond to significant units of our experience; what words, phrases, texts, or mere utterances are signs pointing toward orders of value. These areas are shifting, impermanent, and revise themselves as we get older. But within the individual and his changes they preserve a kind of stability.

The kinds of language which the individual finds meaningful will to some extent be those proposed to him by his own culture, of which of course he is himself partly the creator. But they will be those kinds as he is prepared to, and does, authenticate them by his own life. Works of literature are especially carefully put together units of language which we learn to like or dislike, assert or deny, through a long period of training in the use and consumption of language. In general, as hundreds of critics have said, we tend to receive our literary canon with value tags attached. But the canon is small, a narrow spine of chosen eminences in the vast ocean of literature.

The unbaptized works that meet us, and which we need, from the very first contact spring into the life of familiar signs. In the case of the new work of literature those signs are likely to be highly organized—highly compressed and fused, as Coleridge said —and to betray their debts, freshnesses, and implications with particular speed to those prepared to read them. This is the case with Herondas, provided one has some training in Greek and some little knowledge of the Hellenistic world. (Unusual qualifications, but then every text sets its prerequisites.) Given these qualifications one, from the beginning, will be risking himself forward onto not totally unknown waters. This will especially be the case in works, like those of Herondas, whose shortness includes a fairly rapid establishment of tone and argument.

I found risking forth onto Herondas complex, puzzling, and engaging from the outset. These discoveries were confirmed by rereadings. That confirmation was not, could not, be of the sort that from it the mimes acquired some stable value-traits, some characteristics which from that time on needed no longer to be won back into them. Confirmation simply involved finding a taste, and a pattern of sign-reading, deepening around me and working back over me. Because that happened I took on Herondas, and let him take me on. What I made of the decision, similarly, can have no value which doesn't need continually to be won back into what I can say about these texts.

In other words the answer to the question why one as critic commits himself to the writings of x is almost, but *importantly not entirely*, that one simply commits oneself to those writings. The same analysis can be made for the activity of anyone who attempts to read such a book of crticism.

V

Within the continuity of the personal affirmation of Herondas, here, lies the discovery of the various other continuities I mentioned earlier. That is, the commitment which establishes the personal continuity, mine or yours, makes possible the discovery of those other continuities—between Herondas and his own past, among the members of that small group of us who are students of Herondas, and for whom Herondas thus becomes a past, and between the older and the younger, the living and the dead, the members of that tiny intercommunicating body of scholars of Herondas.

My own decision to establish the personal commitment, which I describe here, was of course not a gratuitous act. Writing on

Archilochos for this same series I found myself wanting to follow that study of the first Greek lyric poet, in fact the earliest extant Western lyric poet, with a study of one of the last ancient Greek poets. It then seemed to me, and still does, that the comparison between the two poets would be telling. I have tried indirectly to probe their interrelationship in the first part of this book. It is one way of measuring the distance gone by Greek poetry between the sixth and the third centuries B.C.

Already before that, however, Herondas had gotten under my skin in the excellent unpublished translations of him made by Richard Emil Braun. I had been struck hard by the genuine and realized modernity of those ten translations, and especially—because Braun emphasized this side of it—by the sense of evil and fall in those translations. I am not now so persuaded by that view of Herondas, but it opened my eyes and made me look. Good translation is a forceful form of criticism.

And before reading those translations? Without making any effort to grow private, where privacy is not in place, I think I can push this account one step farther back, to an outstanding seminar on Theocritos, in which I was taught and taught myself at the University of Texas in 1962. I have never had a more brilliant group of readers and interpreters of ancient Greek around me. But even that is not the essential. Those friends read Theocritos as though he was alive, but also as though he was of another culture. The timeless presence of his tense, ironic, innuendo-filled dialogues pressed on all of us. Yet when the jets from the San Antonio SAC base streamed over our building, we laughed and shuddered at the change of the ages.

That seminar got me into the habit of believing in the existence of Alexandrian poetry.

If there is any salutation I want to close with, here, it is to the living atmosphere of rediscovered Hellenism which I found around me in the Classics Department of the University of Texas, from 1960 to 1964. Co-editing *Arion* magazine was an intense, combative, and often exciting way of rediscovering the closeness of ancient classical culture to modern issues and possibilities. Trying out those possibilities on outstanding and independent students, already men of letters, was equally exciting and bore equally unpredictable fruits. It is a peculiar, bitter, and somehow not surprising fact that the Tower, in which we struggled to grasp the modern world through the ancient, should only a couple of years later have housed the mass killer Charles Whitman, whose demon forced him to threaten the entire modern community of Austin.

Iowa City, Iowa
October, 1970

Contents

Contents

Chronology

Chronology

CHAPTER 1

Herondas: Life and Times

> The fall of Athens meant the end
> of popular art in Greece. C. M.
> Bowra, *Ancient Greek Literature*

WITH Herondas (as with Callimachos or Apollonios Rhodios or with Theocritos, who were his contemporaries) we find ourselves in a world whose whole tone differs radically from that familiar to most admirers of ancient Greece. It may be worthwhile to remind ourselves of certain broad developments which bring us to the threshold of the Alexandrian world in which Herondas lived. When we get to the texts of Herondas it will be possible to take ourselves into those real particulars which give life and substance to the general features of a period. For a beginning, though, we should move in general terms from the better to the less well-known epoch.

I *Early Greek Literature*

With the early Greek Lyric poets of the sixth century B.C.—Archilochos, Solon, Sappho, Tyrtaeos—we are already in an age of transition, of that kind of transition which Herondas cannot have failed to feel in them. Their age was in transition between the ancient-feeling epic world of Homer and Hesiod, and the "modern" world of the fifth century B.C., in which the power and culture of Athens were dominant, and in which social, political, and economic life were all decidedly post-epic and post-heroic.[1]

The transition in question was taking place on several fronts: in political development, in philosophy, and in literature, to mention only three of the many ways in which it is in retrospect possible to carve up that complex unit of human experience.

The political changes were so vast and rapid that even today, when we think back over them, we find ourselves grappling with their implications. It is no wonder that these implications were more than powerful enough still to overwhelm the age of Herondas. We can in fact say of the Alexandrian age, almost as confidently as of earlier ages of Greek culture, that it shows little grasp of the meaning of the periods which preceded it, while at the same time it resonates deeply with the important repercussions of those periods.

What we very approximately call the Homeric Age was politically and socially decentralized. Men lived together in small units, on which they were surrounded by the inevitable poverty and poor housing so standard also in the European Middle Age. Wars were frequent and were fought for causes rising directly from the needs of the feudal units; there was no state, and therefore no general war and no general negotiations. Economy was still based essentially on barter, and, thanks again to the total decentralization, economy still reflected local self-sufficiency. There was at this time not only no Greek world to speak of, but there was nothing like the polis, the city-state, which was to be the dominant political force in the fifth century. Herondas, like every educated Hellene, was familiar with this early condition of his cultural-political heritage (though to what extent and in what way he was familiar with it we can only guess).[2]

It is not far-fetched to draw the philosophy and literature of the epic world into the same field of explanation as the political situation of the time. Surely the later Greeks experienced all these features of early Greece as a single unit of historical awareness. The philosophy of Homer, and of the now misty poets of the epic cycle, is, as far as we know, deeply rooted in their contemporary political experience, is in fact one with it. (By their philosophy I mean that part of their conceptual thought which is not simply a source of our knowledge of their political world.) What they tell us of man, of his relations to his fellow men, and of his gods suggests what the epic political world would lead us to expect; that man in the Homeric age thought of himself and his fellows in class-categories, that he assigned values to himself and others on the basis of honor and often highly sophisticated prowess, and that the Homeric pantheon is a startlingly close reproduction of Homeric society itself, with its internecine quarrels, its decentralized power, and its strong adherence to the world of male competition.

In the world of *arete* (manly excellence; the key moral term in early Greek thought) that which most deeply found its way into the early Greek epic was a certain care for objectivity, for events projected outward from their narrative subjectivity, for characters with sharp outline, clear delineation; finally, for a verse style and form which was marked by disciplined—though subtly varied—regularity, and by an oral-semantic tone which always sounds to us more like proclamation than like ordinary speech. There is no lack of verbal sophistication in Greek epic; any reader of Homer in Greek knows that. It is a question of degree and kind of projection of language, and of its relationship to the subject projecting it. In this sense we might say that Homer's language is highly projected. This projection was of incalculable importance in establishing a ground tone for later Greek literature. The whole basis of the classical is laid here.

Politically, philosophically, and in literature, the immediately post-Homeric world shows much that was new then, and that, from our present perspective, can be considered transitional. (We can be sure that this "perspective" was present, at least as a condensed awareness, in a poet like Herondas, who is in his work so responsible both to the epic and the lyric strands of his literary heritage; and who so regularly refers back into that heritage.) The gradual growth of the polis, the city-state, was the central political fact, one that only slowly and in widely scattered developments made itself felt. The world of feudal decentralization gave way—in the eighth, seventh, and sixth centuries—to the world of Athens, Sparta, Thebes, Euboia, and to all that was involved in the birth of new social communities. These were centuries during which men were still at the beginning of something new; of sophisticated coinage systems; of representative government; of adequate and consistent laws to fit the new systems of government which were appearing. It was also a time during which the individual was finding new opportunities to develop as an individual. This point can be misleading. We are not speaking about an age of individualism. Nor have we any reason to believe that the Homeric age, at its best and most equitable, suppressed the individual; it was, after all, an "age of heroes."

We come at this time, in the sixth century, to those Greeks whom today we consider the first philosophers: Thales, Anaximander, Anaximenes, and their many followers. If man was very generally gaining control, in the new world of the polis, over his own social and political destiny; if he was beginning to define himself more thoughtfully against his world; then nowhere were those moves toward the rational and intelligent more conspicuous than in the Milesian philosophers. They made it their business to ask what kind of world they were in and who they were in this world.

The first lyric poets—Archilochos, Solon, Sappho, Tyrtaeos—were, as I said in opening this historical discussion, living in a time of transition. Of course, their time did not present itself to them in this way, in this form. They no more supposed their age one of transition than the Burgundian of the thirteenth century thought he was living in the Middle Ages. Yet in a sense it is proper to use the notion of transition here.

By being what they were those poets opened new possibilities for the men who followed them; and they brought those possibilities out of their experience of the world which preceded them. What were the lyric poets that they could do this? They were parts of the language of their time, were made possible by it, and were at the same time factors in making it possible and real, in making it a factor in establishing the character of the epoch. To say that these men were individualists is not to say that they were, even as far as we can know them in their poetry, eccentrics, oddities, or even wise distortions from the norm of the Western Personality. They were significant human creators who interposed, between themselves and their audiences, far less protective verbal material than did the Greek epic poets, than do any epic poets. In this the lyric poets resembled their philosopher contemporaries, whose determining characteristic it would also be possible to find, though in a different sense, in their readiness to speak directly into intellectual-existential problems, and through those into that always slightly nebulous audience in terms of which both the lyric poet and the philosopher always negotiate.

II *The Fifth Century*

The fifth century in many ways displays ancient Greek culture to finest advantage, and reveals itself as a broad and total synthesis of much of the development which had grown so powerfully during the preceding five centuries. For this reason we learn unusually much, not only about Greek culture but about human culture, when we get inside the world of fifth-century Greece, of course especially of fifth-century Athens. We also put ourselves in control of the only perspective from which it is possible to look clearly onto the Alexandrian world.

In the most finely developed city-states of the fifth century, in Athens, Sparta, and Thebes, something has come to flower for the growth of which both the feudal epic world and the individualistic early polis were necessary seeds. The epic world's emphasis on deeds, *arete*, combat, and existence in the public dimension are all preserved. They are landmarks of the fifth-century polis. But that polis at its best, especially in Athens, has by the fifth century acquired a kind of interiority, conscience, and self-awareness which if far from totally realized is nonetheless without precedent in ancient political life, and which is far deeper than any form of society that had preceded it in the West. Athenian democracy at its best, and the political life of the other *poleis* in their ways and degrees, took a long step toward bringing that interiority into unity with the clearly self-presenting inheritances from the epic world.

Philosophy, too, is in fifth-century Athens a synthesis, while it is at the same time a restless advance. If we look at what might strictly be called philosophy, at the thought of Xenophanes or Anaxagoras, we find cosmology in which the objective wisdom of epic thought has in some way passed into and through the deepening, and far more private, metaphysical thought of the Milesians. If we look at the hard aspects of the thought of Herodotos or Thucydides, of Aeschylos, Sophocles, or Euripides, we see a comparable development. In them too there is a great fund of public wisdom, a kind of inherited, objectifying sense of man's place in his world, the kind of mode of world-vision from which, in the broadest sense, we imagine Homer too to have worked out. Yet there is also, in the historians and dramatists considered exclusively as thinkers, an interiority which we never find in Homer or Hesiod or the poets of the epic cycle. (We never find it, presumably, because Homer at least had no desire to offer it to us.) It is this interiority, this remarkable quality of thinking objectively but thinking with individuality, which marks the fifth-century synthesis in thought.

Nietzsche has suggested where we should look for the fifth century synthesis in literature. In *The Birth of Tragedy* he says that the spirits of form (the Apollonian) and deep content (the Dionysian) meet in fifth-century tragedy, form serving to contain and to make endurable the too intense awareness of our situation as human beings. In two ways what he says hardly applies to the whole point here. He is considering only tragedy, and he is not thinking, when he speaks of the Dionysian, of the subjectivity of the lyric age. With a little expansion, however, his suggestions can be made to fit the present point helpfully. Fifth-century drama and lyric poetry (Pindar, Bacchylides) can very well be viewed as amalgams of a double legacy: of one tradition, especially an epic tradition, in which form in the broadest and deepest sense was brought to perfection; of another tradition, to which the lyric world came closest, in which the deepest and least conventionalized demands of subjectivity got a hearing.

III *The Fourth Century*

When trying to understand the Alexandrian world it is a convention, but a useful one, to think back to the matters discussed here. It is one small gesture we can make toward getting inside the historical consciousness of the Alexandrian writer. We can probably date the existence of that new breed of writer to the beginning of the fourth century. Of course what we call the Alexandrian world, strictly speaking, does not begin until the third century, but there is some value in thinking of the fourth century as already standing apart from the periods described above. There is unquestionably a dialectical fullness to the growth of Greek culture from 1000 to 400 B.C. No formula, such as that of thesis, antithesis, and synthesis can be more than a rude guide to organization, when it comes to material both so rich and, in another sense, so relatively thinly documented. Yet such a formula can help us to see that there is a kind of unity in the cultural work being done in those six hundred years. (Though the mind is staggered at a generalization like this, which wraps up six hundred years in a sentence, still it is one of the necessary ways in which we think.)

Again Nietzsche helps us to understand this matter, with his original and devastating hatred of Socrates and of the Socratic mind; that hatred which he works out of himself at some detail in the second part of *The Birth of Tragedy*. (Leszek Kolakowski, in *The Alienation of Reason,* discusses in connection with Positivism the surprising relevance of hating to thought which is creative and perceptive; that is a good gloss on the situation with Nietzsche.) For Nietzsche the period opened by Homer and closed by Euripides is somehow a whole, and enjoys a confidence and integrity of its own. Euripides and Socrates are the first "great questioners," impudent rationalists who break in upon this unity with their superficial pursuit of wisdom. The culture which preceded them, and which they helped to erode, had a strength and assurance which they could not imagine.

Whatever we think of Nietzsche's thesis, it enables us to localize a certain sense of loss, of decline, perhaps even of sadness, which finds itself into Greek art, thought, and political life after 400 B.C. and much more after 300 B.C. I am of course describing this situation in the broadest and most general terms. But when we come to grips with Herondas it will be useful to have such generalities as a background. It will be useful when we come to Herondas, a poet lacking that *Heiterkeit und Allgemeinheit*, that *joy* and *general* or *universal* quality which the German tradition has always thought it could find in fifth-century and earlier Hellenism. (The particular phrase is from Winckelmann, the great art-historian who used it in his *History of Art in Antiquity* to describe the highest quality of Apolline fifth-century statuary.)

The "sadness" in question is already apparent, in its deeply different expressions, in Plato, Theophrastos, and Menander, three somehow representative figures of the fourth century. (It will be seen at once that "sadness" is to be understood here as "sense of loss," an often indefinable but very real sense.) In Plato, for the first time in Greek culture, we see a strongly expressed longing for the "ideal" which is superior to the real. This is true in Plato's epistemological thought as well as in his theology, or in his metaphysical thought. The epistemology with which we are most familiar, from dialogues like the *Meno, Parmenides,* or *Theaetetos,* is based on a thoroughgoing search for the grounds of intelligibility, the conditions which make knowing possible. The knowing of the particular details, of the reality into which human existence plunges us, is possible only because the intelligibility of those details is guaranteed by their "ideas." The "idea" of tree, for example, has an independent existence which guarantees the intelligibility of the particular tree. Plato's theology carries this kind of concern, of which I give only the crudest indication here, one level higher, and diffracts it in several directions. In that theology the body is only the container of the soul, a higher principle which visits bodies. (There are unmistakable resonances of Indian thought in this.) The self is itself homeless in this world, and yearns—in some ways like the Christian soul—for its home in another world. One might even say, looking to the late dialogue *Timaeos,* that for Plato the whole cosmos embodied a certain yearning for the total order potential and inherent in it. This would be the ultimate in "sadness" of the kind I am discussing; a universal, cosmic sadness. But it is not necessary to go so far with the present argument. The speculative audacity of the Milesian philosophers is their way of affirming the positive presence of the world; they try to interpret the puzzling appearance under which reality presents itself, and they tend to carry out their interpretations metaphorically, in terms, say, of water, air, or fire. But Plato's audacity is not interpretive in that sense; he explains given reality from a level of being which is above it and entirely independent from it.

Theophrastos and Menander belong to Plato's century. (Plato died in 347 B.C., Theophrastos in 287 B.C., and Menander in 291 B.C.) When we look back to the portrayals of human nature which we find in Greek epic, tragedy, and even history, we find assumptions and perceptions about human nature which are only less obvious in Theophrastos's *Characters* and Menander's plays. Or, more exactly, the emphasis is different in those later works. The changed emphasis is the source of a kind of sadness comparable to the sadness in Plato.

The new world is a bourgeois world, at least in its earlier stages. The characters who fascinate Theophrastos are the ordinary, though generalized and typical, characters who crowd the streets of the growing cities of the Hellenistic world: we see the ironical man, the flatterer, the talker, the skinflint, the boor, the bore, and many others. (In some ways it is a Dickensian gallery.) There are naturally no heroes on this stage. But even the figures presented are seen through a diminishing lens. We have something here quite different from depreciation of characters, what Aristotle called "making men appear worse than they are," in Attic comedy. In Aristophanes there is a distortion and heightening of the portrayed ridiculous characters, which takes them sharply, almost surrealistically, out of life, and puts them squarely into literature.

But in Theophrastos, although there is some comic distortion, there is a closeness to the details of observed "middle-class" existence, which makes one feel that not only the age of heroism but the age of literary heightening is in the past. The perspective of Theophrastos is close to our own, and may seem the most natural to us. Many people teaching Humanities to American undergraduates have found that they can lead a student into Theophrastos much more easily than into Aeschylos, Euripides, or Thucydides. The greatest authors of the fifth century are often inaccessible for us. Part of the problem is their deep habit of heightening.

We feel the same closeness to Menander and his plays. His plays are drawing-room, or anyway marketplace, comedies, which like Theophrastos's work direct themselves to idealized or typified representations of daily life. There is nothing heroic, much that is anti-heroic, and a general social concern that contents itself with pointing out the foibles and aspirations of mankind. More than one successful soap opera is latent in Menander's work, and more than one was extracted from it by Terence. It is easy to see why we feel at home in this literature.

Where is the bond between Plato and these contemporary sociologists, Theophrastos and Menander; how, once more, do all these men mark themselves off from their happier predecessors? Do the notions of sadness and loss still help us here?

A certain sadness, a sense of departed glory, unmistakably reveals itself in the world-picture of Menander and Theophrastos. This is the sadness which Plato, and Socrates before him, had felt, and from which they had turned toward ideas and ideals. In Menander and Theophrastos we see pictures of the world from which Plato turned his eyes, the world of the cave. It is not an evil world which we see here; it is in a sense far less evil, and less potentially disastrous, than that envisaged by Aeschylos, Sophocles, or Thucydides. But the fourth-century literary world is fallen, has gradually become the secular world unrelieved by any inner sense of how to transcend itself, unless perhaps it would be by casting up, onto its own surface, representative and typical figures in whom general traits of the human condition would be perceptible.

The sense of loss which I am describing here—hastily and as a spiritual background—bore directly onto the world of Herondas himself; and it came to him not just in literary tradition, but in the affairs of the polis, which was rapidly expanding into the large city of the new, international, Hellenistic world, that world which was in many senses so modern, with its

trouble of prices and wages; Socialism and Communism, the strike and the revolution; the growth of ideas of humanity and brotherhood combined with savage quarreling; the emancipation of woman and restriction of population; questions of franchise and (possibly) representation, of emigration and the proletariat; exact learning and crass superstition side by side . . . the spread of education, resulting in the manufacture of masses of the half-educated; the more conscious emergence of propaganda; the growth of all the half-worlds that cling to the skirts of science, of history, and of religion.[3]

The unity of the fifth-century city-state at its best, as in Athens, had been shattered; in fact the Peloponnesian War, the fifth-century Greek civil war, had thoroughly disrupted the entire political unity of the Greeks. It is leaving out much, but stating the essential, to say that the fourth century was a period of self-appraisal during which the Greek polis prepared itself for the totally new political conception which Alexander had in store for it. Newer cities like Greek Thebes gained power; older ones like Athens lost it. Alexander stretched out the Greek world to the Indus River. Yet, if I am not mistaken, a sense of loss found itself even into that enlarged world. By trying to make that statement more precise here, we bring ourselves directly to Herondas the Alexandrian.

IV   Herondas and the Alexandrian World

With Herondas, as with his contemporaries Callimachos, Lycophron, and Theocritos, we are in a world which has already for some time been part of the post-Alexander world state. At Alexander's death (323) his empire was divided up by the ambitious, and often great, generals who had helped to make him powerful. To simplify: Ptolemy gained control of Egypt, Seleucos of Babylon and Syria, Antigonos (at first) of Asia Minor, and Antipater of Macedonia. Despite massive subsequent shufflings these large subareas of empire were to remain essentially intact for several hundred years. The absorption of this entire world into the Roman imperium came only slowly and gradually. Egypt, in 30 B.C., was the last to go.

The civilization of Egypt which followed the death of Alexander was quite unlike any known before, and was represented to perfection by its chief city, Alexandria. That metropolis was one of the first international conurbations: a center of all kinds of trade, of religions from East and West, of literary sophisticates (from all places), and of political intrigue. There had been nothing remotely like this in the world of the polis.

We know nothing concrete about Herondas's relation to this world except that he is somewhere in what he wrote, and what he wrote appears to offer a faithful picture of many aspects of Alexandrian society in the third century, as well, of course, as offering many interrelations with the cultural situation of that time. The "faithful picture" he offers is at the same time his evidence for the kind of historical sadness which I have been attributing here to the creative literature of his period.

Apart from the few details we can conjecture of Herondas's life, that he was probably from the island of Cos, probably lived in Alexandria itself for some time, probably flourished during the first half of the third century B.C.; apart from these details, to which we will return later, Herondas is known chiefly for his mimes, short dramatic dialogues or playlets in which he brings into mutual confrontation conspicuous lower or middle-class character types of the Alexandrian world of his day: pimps, petty schoolmasters, ordinary housewives, slaves, cobblers, and others.[4] There is nothing "ennobling" about these characters in themselves, their actions, their statements, or the way they relate to each other; nor is there anything ennobling, though there is much that is human, in the way Herondas presents his entire offering of this world to us. We seem to be meeting, in highly sophisticated verse form, characters off the streets, or out of the most commonplace living rooms. This is no longer the world of the fifth century, hardly that of the fourth. (It is interesting to see how much more distanced than this, and in that sense how much heightened, are even the sharply attacked characters who interest Aristophanes: Cleon or Socrates.) With Herondas we are in a period of historical fall, historical sadness, at least in one sense. But that is still to say very little.

It is at least to say, in the case of an historically erudite poet like Herondas, who was living at a late stage of his culture's development, that in him there will be much that is retrospective; and

that in his retrospection there will be much half-awakened awareness of his cultural past. In the preface I mentioned the foreshortening, jamming, and asymmetrical characteristics of one's own
cultural past, as it is experienced inwardly and privately; all this
and more bears here. In Herondas's case—in addition to his "sadness" and his general tone of retrospection—there will be further
ramifications which in historical perspective take us back into
much of the material discussed earlier here.

I have so far spoken of Herondas's writings, and those of his
contemporaries, even of certain of his fourth-century predecessors, as embodying a kind of nostalgia for the earlier Greek world;
the kind of nostalgia a contemporary dramatist, say, might feel for
the more wholehearted world of Elizabethan drama.

This is not a unitary nostalgia, directed toward an undifferentiated block of the past, a notion of history which keeps creeping
into our language but has little to do with our real perception of
our past; rather this is a response, in the educated fourth-century
Greek writers as well as in Herondas, to the complex, three-stage
growth which earlier Greek culture represents. To know toward
what Herondas felt back, in his complicated and resonant mimes,
we need to know about the epic, lyric, and dramatic worlds, from
the tenth through the fifth centuries, which preceded him. (We
naturally think of "preceding," while he, of course, would have
thought of it more as a question of "existing in him.") Later it will
be easy enough to show, in detail, why this is true: from the evidence of the linguistic, philosophical, and broadly cultural traces
left, in Herondas's poetry, by its forerunners.

There is another way in which it is essential to see Herondas in
terms of his tradition; and this time we are forced to exercise our
own historical imaginations in a difficult but useful way. There is
much in common between the first Greek lyric poets, those of the
sixth century like Archilochos, Solon, and Sappho, and the later
Greek poets, those of the third century like Theocritos, Callimachos, and Herondas. In both cases the poetry of lyric subjectivity
is being written in a kind of opposition to, or resistance against, a
more objectifying and more classical age; in one case against the
age of Homeric (and many other) epics, in the other against that
of fifth century Athenian literature, of that drama and history
which we have long considered to be classical in the sense of per-
fected and permanent. In each age of lyric expression the need for

personal statement is strongly felt and strongly expressed. Herondas needs to comment on the intimacies of life, as he experiences them, as much as Archilochos does, though the different ways in which they do this say volumes about the differences between their two ages. It is at least geometrically interesting to think of the two "lyric" ages of Greece as bracketing between them the more consolidated and strikingly less lyrical fifth-century achievement. And it is probably more interesting than that. The matter probably takes us close to the question of rhythms and cycles in literary history, but that question is too broad for the present discussion.

Finally we need, in this preliminary setting-of-context, to be sure that we see the gross differences between Herondas and his contemporaries and the earlier Greek lyric poets. Without some sense of those earlier poets we could not be aware of this difference, and it is for that reason, too, that we must constantly refer back in time from Herondas. As a sampling of this difference we can think about how differently the earlier lyricists presented their "I," themselves as subjectivity.

The sixth-century lyricists seem to burst forth with the first personal pronoun, after the "repression" of the objectifying epic age. This is an exaggerated way to put it; it is a question of contrast with the tone of the ancient epic. It is also, however, a question of contrast with Hellenistic poetry. Theocritos, Herondas, and Callimachos are no longer lyric poets in the earlier sense; in fact they live in a world which produced no more lyric poetry, as far as we can tell from the remaining documents. (No more lyric poetry in the strictest Greek sense, that is; though today in English we might call some of it lyric.) It is of course no longer a question, with these lyric poets, of the "I" being submerged by the weight of an epic world. The burden of epic repression is nearly gone. Even Callimachos, who wrote learned epic poetry (the *Argonautica*), is present in his poems in a way which would have been both impossible and unnatural to Homer. Herondas is far more present; although in his brief mimes he is careful not to intrude as poet, we are conscious everywhere of the poet's intimate, guiding, conversing tone.

In one way we feel closer to Herondas, as a personality in his poems, than we do to Archilochos or Sappho. This is partly a question of our age's relation to that of Herondas. We too exist in

a late stage of a culture's history, perhaps toward the end of Western Christian-Classical culture, at least in any familiar form of
that culture; and in our stage we feel both a fascination with our
fall and a nostalgia for our past, a nostalgia which readies us to
feel sympathy for Herondas and his world-perspective. (To be
very selectively specific, I think our nostalgia is deeply felt in the
work of Rilke, Valéry, Eliot, and Cavafis.) When we look back to
the first Greek lyric poets we meet a freshness and excitement, at
the discovery of how to express, how to name and use, subjectivity
in poetry; and this excitement we can no longer do more than
admire and appreciate. The pride with which Archilochos informs
us, in a delicious, frank couplet, that he is both a soldier of Ares
and a lover of the Muses, echoes down to us from the earlier strata
of our own historical consciousness. I am afraid that in our conscious minds we can hear and understand, only too well, some
implied "so what" on the lips of an Herondas.

V   *Herondas's Life and Work*

The relation between Herondas's work and his private life, his
daily biography, is as obscure as is that relation in the case of most
ancient Greek writers. In a sentence, earlier, I stated the main
known facts of that life; and in many paragraphs, in my preface, I
suggested some of the consequences of this situation. When we
come down to cases the ancient relation of life-works is obscure
because we know almost nothing firm about the lives of those
men, or because what we know is only gossip, rumor, and myth,
the ancient substitutes for biography or autobiography. For this
reason, though also for others, I have opened my effort to set a
context for Herondas's work with a fairly wide historical pano-
rama. It is in fact the most relevant frame in which to set Herondas's pictures of third-century life.

How true this is we see when we come closer toward the relation of life to works. It is too little to say that we know virtually
nothing about Herondas's life. Prior to 1890, when the papyrus
containing much of Herondas's text was first published, we knew
of this poet's existence only through some ten indirect references
in ancient authors, mainly Latin authors. (And as a matter of fact
those references contained almost as many different spellings of
the poet's name, confusing him once with Herodotos, and tending
to favor what is probably the correct orthography, *Herodas:* it is a

canonized accident, apparently, that we write *Herondas,* as we can see from the detailed discussions in the Knox-Headlam or Puccioni editions of Herondas's work.) Number 135 in the British Museum's collection of papyri gave a new poet to the world. In that papyrus, about which I will say more in a moment, were found the nine early complete poems which will be discussed in the next chapter; and which, though brief (85 to 129 lines in length), constitute the remaining opus of this poet. Each of those poems, mimes, is a little play offering, as I have said, a scene or type-characterization from contemporary Alexandria. The poems are turned outward from the poet; they do not express his subjectivity directly, but only indirectly through his observations of the social world. For this reason we do not get to know Herondas "personally" in his poems. But for the same reason we do not get to know his society or human surrounding concretely through his poems, though that surrounding is in some sense observed in these poems. This is a difficult but important point about Herondas's poetry, as it is about that of Theocritos or Callimachos or any of the other major Alexandrian writers. Those men concealed themselves subtly in the highly sophisticated folds of their works, and for that reason, because they stayed out of the surface of their own works, they offered only highly generalized versions of the worlds they lived in, and no versions at all of their own lives. In a literary age such as the Alexandrian, literary and cultural tradition is the most reliable context for understanding a man's literary works.

Since we are dealing here with a born poet, however, we will find that "literary and cultural tradition" is part of his life, a most important part of it. The fact that we have no biographical evidence about him is frustrating but not disastrous; not as disastrous as it would have been, for example, in the case of a military man or of a man of state.

CHAPTER 2

The Texts Themselves

> *Things that are morally shocking in Herondas come to the fore so crudely that one cannot deny the importance of morality for him.* Bruno Snell, *Poetry and Society*

IT is sobering to look into Papyrus 135 in the British Museum Collection, at that roll of stiff papyrus which is our chief evidence not only for the poetry but for the existence of Herondas. It is moving to see so much confined on one sheet, "five meters in length, 12.4 centimeters in height, with 46 columns which vary from a minimum height of 8 centimeters to a maximum of 8.5 centimeters." [1] It is even moving—and I think we can discover the reasons for that later—to see how small and clear the writing is, and to learn that it seems to be in a hand of the first century after Christ: "some corrections, in cursive, seem to be from the second century after Christ . . ." [2] (Puccioni, ix). Without this material evidence, as I said, we would be confined for our knowledge of Herondas to the ten or so ancient references to him.

The sobering of the first look results from this: we are simply struck by the age and fragility of the document, by realizing again the slimness of the reed by which so much ancient literature is sustained. The discussion of this particular reed turns up at first the kind of information already given here. Second and then further looks at the papyrus have led the best editors, like Knox, well beyond the basic facts, that the text can be dated to early Ptolemaic Egypt and that the scribe's work belongs to the "first century or the first half of the second century" after Christ. We learn from Knox that the codex writing is "not the work of a highly trained scribe," that "not only was he [the scribe] prone to all the common errors of copyists but worst of all he suffered from a schoolboy

42

knowledge of Greek, and, where he followed the sense roughly, made, unconsciously, stupid alterations." [3] It will be appropriate, occasionally in the following pages, to discuss some of the very practical consequences, for the understanding of Herondas's texts, which result from these scribal uncertainties. For the moment we only need to consider how fragile the identity of those texts generally is.

I *Herondas and the Mime*

The form in which Herondas wrote, in which he adopted toward the Hellenic cultural past the attitude and stances described in the last chapter, was the mime, referred to earlier and called by the Greeks the *mimiambos*, a playlet or mime written in iambic verse. There is an historical context for that form.

Sicily and Magna Grecia were the first homes of the Greek mime. The early Greek literature of those regions, especially that of the poet Sophron, in the mid-fifth century, is full of folk wit and earthy language; at least to judge from the preserved fragments, which are "so scanty that they give no notion of the contents and form," but only of the fundamental linguistic tone. Sophron appears to have been the first to bring these raw materials into something like literary form. Evidently, his influence made itself widely felt in the Greek world; we hear of a number of *mimiambi*, mime-writers, following him, men like Sciras (of Tarentum), Blaesus, one Xenarchus (of Rhegium in South Italy); we also learn about Plato's admiration for Sophron's dramatic techniques, and that under Plato's pillow, at his death, comedies of Aristophanes and mimes of Sophron were found. The names of Sophron's followers are, unfortunately, only names to us now: Sophron is only a little more. But if he entered into the conception of Plato's dialogues, he is in a sense much more than a name.

The most important literary development from these early mimes—besides the work of Herondas—is that of Herondas's contemporary Theocritos. Here we must speak of development from, rather than direct continuation of, the tradition of the mime. The idylls of Theocritos are pastoral, highly literary, and strictly formalized in the personal relationships they dramatize. As art-works they preserve a great deal more distance from reality than do mimes, and they display no interest in the somewhat fallen bourgeois reality which is the world of the mime. However, in the

larger spectrum of ancient Greek literary forms the idyll and the
mime are close (as both of them are in a sense to the Hellenistic
play). They are brief—one to two hundred line—dramatizations
of small scenes, among characters (whether bucolic or urban)
drawn from daily contemporary life. The language is in both cases
inclined to archaism; and to difficult reuses both of more ancient
and of dialectal expressions. The noble, the edifying, and the philosophical are in both subgenres reduced to a minimum. The fifteenth idyll of Theocritos, to which I will return later, is a particularly good point of comparison with Herondas.

The language, the meter, the content or substance of Herondas's mimes all rest on thoroughly worked-out, though sometimes
hard to trace, precedents. It is almost impossible for us to put
ourselves back into the organic unity of the ancient Greek language, at any point in its history; but this act of historical empathy is entirely impossible when we reach a late stage of the
Greek language, such as that in which Herondas adds himself to
the history of Greek. By that stage there is no cohesion between
literary and colloquial language. The "language of ordinary men,"
in Alexandria, was a Greek which had already begun to lose many
of the distinguishing marks of the classical language: its careful
systems of conjugation and declension; its immense and highly
differentiated vocabulary; its capacity for abstraction. Alexandrian men of letters were consequently more than usually forced
back, for this and other reasons, to the language of their great fifth-
century models. This return to the past is the source of an un-
precedented interweaving, in writers like Herondas, Callimachos,
and Theocritos, of the language of their own time with elegant
archaisms. This situation is unlike any intimately known to us in
our position within twentieth-century English, though both James
Joyce and Ezra Pound provide us with some examples of this
strategy.

Herondas turns back to a distinctive brand of Ionic Greek, the
kind of Greek generally associated with Attica and the highest
culture of Athens, but widely spoken thoughout the earlier Hellenic world, and concentratedly spoken on the Asia Minor coast.
In particular, he turns to the Ephesian Ionic which was used by
Hipponax, a mid-sixth century satirist known to us from antiquity
as the "father of parody," and as such influential on Herondas in a
more than verbal way. As far as the linguistic archaism goes here,

"antique Ionic, with Herondas, extends to little more than his vocabulary: the cast and construction of his sentences is for the most
part fluent Attic; he is thinking in the style of Attic comedy, then
translating words or phrases into what he considers to be their
antique equivalents, not always with perfect accuracy." [4] Headlam gives us a list of several such "antiqued" expressions, with
their standard Attic equivalents: Herondas will write "he drags
along his age" for "he feels heavy," "blowing in their beards" for
"breathing," "washing his tongue in honey" for "dipping his
tongue." Such examples, of course, show us Herondas at his most
artificial. On the whole, as Headlam says, the style in Herondas is
fluent Attic.

The linguistic traditionalism in Herondas goes much farther
than this, and in some of its details we can see a great deal that
leads us deeply into this poet. A certain stylization marks his language in the lexical archaisms just mentioned; it extends to his
apparently self-conscious use of proverbs, to his favoring of high-
style synonyms instead of "usual" words, to his way of naming his
characters, even to his broad reliance on "character types," the
basis of his whole literary perception. (This last issue brings us to
Herondas's philosophy or ideas, but also to precisely the point
where his position in language becomes something more than
that; where, to anticipate, it becomes a certain self-conscious distancing perception of the human world as divisible into personality groups.) Finally, still on the preliminary level of technical traditionalism, we will have to say something about Herondas's
metrics.

Of the use of proverbs and "high-style" synonyms, there is little
of general importance to say beyond what was said about his use
of Ionic dialect, for that usage, in its self-consciousness and literary
distancing, is characteristic of Herondas's entire operation in language. Like other Alexandrian writers he uses proverbs to give a
common and earthy tone to his "realism." Yet, as we will see over
and over again, Herondas's "realism" is of a special kind; and precisely in the question of proverbial usage it is special. Headlam
calls attention to one neat and telling example of this. Mime Three,
in which the example is found, deals with a naughty schoolboy
and with the even naughtier upbraiding by his mother; finally
with his punishment by his schoolmaster. At one point the schoolmaster says to the boy:

But you're a bad boy, Kottalos, so bad that none could find a good
word for you even were he selling you, not even *in the land where
mice throughout eat iron.* (Italics mine) (III, 74–76)

The proverb sticks out like a bar of iron here, and seems, on the
schoolmaster's lips, to combine literary reference, even a slightly
phoney erudite tone, with a gritty reality. This tension would in
itself be part of the recipe for Herondas's brand of traditionalism.
It is a traditionalism which uses the contemporary world but ret-
rojects it backward in time. But there is a hidden distancing effect
even in the present example. In Hesiod this proverb would have
fitted organically to the tone of the passage. Hesiod, as a *persona*
in his kind of epic poetry, was able to express himself naturally in
the way the schoolmaster does here. But Herondas is too "sophisticated" to manage that tone, even as a piece of slightly erudite
archaism, without adding more to it. In the present case his use of
traditionalized language adds to his whole passage an irony, and
an *attention to itself as language,* which are supremely distancing.

Herondas's way of naming his characters is also a way of
achieving an effect of distance. (I am intentionally not trying to
define "distancing effect" as I go along; the classic discussion, on
which I am essentially relying here, is in Bullough's "Psychical
Distance"; there is a good extension of the argument in Suzanne
Langer's *Mind: An Essay on Feeling.*) It is at the same time a
projection toward the past. Like Menander and Theophrastos,
Herondas often gives his characters almost directly significant
names—Kerdon (Greedy), Gastron (Paunchy), or Threissa
(Thracian). This convention leads directly into a broadly conceptual development of the individual mimes. The projection is into
the literary-historical past, and one of its effects is to counteract
any personal engagement between mime-reader (or watcher, if
that was the case) and the characters represented in the mime.

Far more to the present point, though related, is Herondas's
whole preference for type-characters. Here too he joins Theophrastos and Menander, and for the simple reason that he, like
them, is experiencing and representing the world generally in his
language. He also joins, at an earlier stage, the authors of Attic
comedy and of those Sicilian mimes which generated so much in
Herondas.

The natural way to remember, consider, and reflect on his work is in terms of the type-characters it embodies, and through which he reaches back in spirit to a whole traditional literary perception of human reality. The extant mimes are devoted to the spectrum of characters I mentioned earlier: the bawd, the pander, the schoolmaster, the fussy old woman, the jealous woman, the slave girl, the cobbler; and to a wide diversity of lesser figures, less prominent character-types, subgroups. (Such discussions, even in classical psychological literature, tend to be both useful and vague; as in the classic work on personality types by Adler, a pupil of Freud.) These types will seem to be central to everything we discuss in Herondas's poetic achievement. Everything in him which involves traditional stylization, and a concurrent distancing, can be deduced from his concern with type-characters.

Finally, it is necessary to mention his prosody, though at this point we can hardly do more than draw general attention to it. A more meaningful account of it will have to wait for the next chapter, where we will come to discussing texts. Herondas wrote in choliambic, limping iambic, lines, which end in spondees ($--$), emphatic changes of emphasis. Hipponax, mentioned above, seems to be the father of this line, which thus offers itself as a traditional vehicle and, to the aurally trained and sensitive, as a distancing vehicle; a sharp break, for instance, with contemporary prose, the language of Herondas's day. It is important to know, about the basic poetic vehicle of Herondas's language, how sharp a tension it maintains against the ordinary language of his day; and though when it comes to any ancient "language of the day" we have to speculate, I think we speculate from firm ground. All the linguistic analogies we can bring to bear suggest that in ancient classical languages, as in modern Indo-European languages, the prosodic patterns imposed on poetry, whether iambic, dactylic or spondaic patterns, or any combination of these, were precisely that, patterns; and as such they counteracted the naturally patternless movement of the spoken language.

II *Mime One*

It will be a good idea to discuss the first mime in some detail, for in this way we can put a number of the previous points to work, and can understand something of the character of all Herondas's dramatic pieces. The simple story line is essentially this.

Two women, Metriche (which suggests *mother,* and connotes

the woman of measure) and Threissa (*the Thracian woman*) are
talking in the former's sitting room. Threissa is Metriche's serving
woman. There is a knock on the door. Threissa opens it to reveal
Gyllis, mother of Philainion. Gyllis enters, starts talking with
Metriche, complains of her own aging, and contrasts it with the
still green liveliness of Metriche, who though a widow is ripe for
love—at least in Gyllis's opinion. In fact Gyllis's opinion on that
matter constitutes the main theme of the mime. "Well, my child,"
she says, "how long are you going on in your widowhood, keeping
your own solitary couch? For it's five months since Mandris set sail
to Egypt, and not a line has he sent you. He has forgotten you and
drunk of a new cup" (ll. 21–25). Mandris is in Egypt where there
are more beautiful women than "there are stars in the sky." Therefore, Gyllis says, Metriche should have some pleasure for herself.
This suggestion is flavored with conventional wisdom: "for un-
happy man life is uncertain," so take advantage of the moment.

The second half of the mime centers around Gyllis's proposition. She has been approached by a handsome young man, a fine
athlete and still a virgin, who was terribly struck by Metriche's
beauty when he saw her at a festival. Since that time, says Gyllis,
"he leaves not my house night nor day but weeps over me and
coaxes me and is dying of desire." Metriche should go to this se-
cret lover and satisfy both herself and him. But Metriche is outraged by the suggestion. "Gyllis," she says, "white hair dulls the
mind; for, I swear by Mandris's safe return and by dear Demeter,
I would not willingly have stayed out such a speech from another
woman, but I would have hated henceforward the threshold of
my door" (ll. 67–72). The mime ends, however, on a strange
note. After flatly turning down Gyllis's proposition, Metriche stops
her criticisms with the reflection that this "is not the tale that Gyllis wants to hear: so, Threissa, wipe the cup clean and pour out
three measures of neat wine; dribble some water over it and give
her a good dose" (ll. 78–81). The action of the mime ends with
Gyllis relishing the wine she has been given; a relish which she
expresses with the lecherous gusto of the stock "bawd." The implication of the mime, however, is harder to locate. There is no
doubt, on surface verbal evidence, that Metriche dismissed Gyllis's propostion. But then why *does* Metriche listen through to the
end of the proposition, through the very juicy lines 48–66; and

why, at the end, does she treat Gyllis with wine? There is a nicely unspecified aroma of evil over the mime.

This kind of implication sets the tone of much of Herondas's work, which is rich in innuendo and devoted to the complex ambiguities of ordinary life. Realizing this tone in Herondas can perhaps reintroduce us in a fresh way to some of the points made earlier about Herondas's distancing, and about the aesthetic placing of his work in traditional literary contexts which free the work from the burden of contemporaneity. The implication and innuendo in the first mime bring into it a quality of evil collusion, and dangerous temptation, which heighten its excitement far above that of a realistic genre-sketch. The evil in question is of course not satanic; its pretensions are small but fertile, for the corrosion of personality can be seen successfully at work here.

This whole constructed scene coalesces with the freeing from realism, from a sense of conscious subservience to given details. The scene of the first mime is sharply cut off from the life outside the outer room; from the rumor of the streets, for instance. Within the room we hear obscure hints of the outer world—of Egypt, where is to be found "all that exists and is produced in the world . . . wealth, wrestling grounds, might, peace, renown, shows, philosophies, money, young men, the domain of the Twin-gods [Ptolemy Philadelphos and his wife Arsinoe], the king a good one, the museum, wine, all good things one can desire . . ." (ll. 26-31). During her discussion of Egypt, Gyllis, the proposer of temptations, seems almost a mythical figure. She disappears in and out of Herondas's virtual dedication of his poem to Ptolemy and the Kingdom. In the course of the speech Metriche dwindles away, to reappear at the end, in her half-convincing rebuttal of the proposition. By this time she is almost an alter ego to Gyllis.

The artificiality of the scene established here may be easier to grasp if we look at it in relation to some of those distancing techniques discussed at the beginning of this book. We can do this with an eye to seeing Herondas the artist more clearly; not, of course, to blinding ourselves toward that "realism" which is in some sense the raw material of his whole world: it is obvious that he looks at daily life more closely than any of his predecessors in Greek literature.

Of the Ephesian Ionic character of the Greek language in this

mime there is little appropriate to say, on the level suitable to this
book. The relevant argument is enshrined, for instance, in the
wonderfully rich and detailed footnotes which Headlam appends
to his text and translation of each mime. An examination of that
sort rapidly convinces us of two facts: that the *general* character
of the text is rooted linguistically in a distinctive form of Ionic;
but that the study of specific words leads into innumerable by-
ways, into plays of language, and into historical-cultural innuendoes, of which we would otherwise have had no expectation. The
range of those specific discoveries is vast, and proves to us again—
though we wonder how we ever forgot it—how little we can feel
the cultural associations and resonances of an ancient language,
especially in its poetry. Threissa, the servant girl who speaks with
Metriche at the outset of the mime, is "named for" Thrace, her
country of origin; this kind of nomenclature, for which there was
the widest precedent in ancient literature, must have created a
sharply typifying effect, the effect of putting the girl into a distinct
class. We learn as much as we can about "the descent of Misa" (1.
56), at the festival in honor of which Mandris saw and fell in love
with Metriche; the festival is rooted in obscenities profoundly
connected with Orphism and the cult of Demeter, a connection
which bears directly onto the poetic argument of the mime. (It
opens out the meaning of the mime into implications which have
to remain partly academic for us; but which would have been
most eloquent to a contemporary hearer.) Or, finally and quite
randomly for the sake of example, we learn how complexly literary are the resonances of an expression like (1. 71) "I would have
taught her to sing her lame song with a limp," the assault
Metriche tosses at Gyllis at the end of the latter's proposition. We
find out how much such an expression, which is not a proverb but
basically a literary coinage, could remind an educated Alexandrian of passages in, say, Sophocles or Euripides. The resonances
are complex and familar. Aesthetic counterplay with the past exists at its finest and most direct precisely on this verbal level.

The literary peripheries of Herondas's language are hard for us
to trace; the three samples just offered give a bare suggestion of
that difficulty: they remind us that the language of Herondas had
connotations which were commonly understood in his day, but
which we have to relearn; further, that we cannot relearn those
connotations without doing some homework in the cultural his-

tory which preceded Herondas. The language of Herondas provides more than the usual amount of literary leavening of that immediately given language-world which aspires to reproduce "real" daily life directly. One of the examples, the simplest, was that of the name *Threissa;* it took us into the next question, of the stylization in naming, which is part of Herondas's literary heritage and literary strategy. The effect of calling that servant-girl "the Thracian" was to generalize the experience of her in the mime, where "generalize" means to place her back in her *genus,* to draw attention away from whatever is most specific about her. She is, of course, so minor a character, even in this small piece, that we cannot hope to conclude much from the example. What about Metriche and Gyllis? There is much less to go on here. (The exceptional being a useful reminder, in this case, that interpretation of literary works will never fit comfortably into a pattern.) Headlam gives us little hope with Metriche, a name occurring in one inscription, and formally "a Doric diminutive of *Metris.*" Of *Metris* he has, with his caution, characteristically little to say. I wonder, though, whether we can't hear two obvious echoes in the name, which would have been set ringing in the literary Alexandrian ear? There is the echo of *mētēr* (mother) and that of *metron* (meter or measure or limit). These two senses work together to enrich and generalize our perception of Metriche's character, where "enrich" means to extend and make more comprehensive, rather than to fill with more sensuous detail, another possible sense of "enrichment" here. If we accept the ironic tone, which I find at the end of the mime, the idea of Metriche as measure-mother will seem especially piquant, and in a way that does nothing but add to the literary energy of the piece. It is at least possible that the Greek literary ear, which was far more accustomed than the modern ear to hearing the meanings in the roots of names, would have taken in all these connotations of the woman's name. The name *Gyllis* gives us less to go on, and what it gives through scholarship it may well not have given to any of Herondas's contemporary readers. This is a familiar possibility to students of Greek, or any ancient literature; and it illustrates the limits of scholarship and the need for scholarly tact. The present instance is exactly to the point. *Gyllís,* with the accent on the last syllable, is a new name, without precedent in Greek literature; but there are several instances, in Xenophon for example, of the same

name in its masculine form, with the accent (either acute or cir-
cumflex) on the first syllable. There is enough of the masculine in
Gyllis herself to give even this overtone its relevance. There is one
more choice overtone, a tidbit and a possibility, found this time,
as so often in later Greek, in Hesychios's *Lexikon,* that treasure
house of linguistic peculiarities compiled in the fourth century A.D.
Gulios is in Hesychios given as the "name of Herakles the great
eater." How widely known that epithet was, we have now no way
to guess. If it was known, its bearing on and relevance to the
unlovable Gyllis can be imagined. Our picture of significant naming, in Herondas, would be filled out a little farther.

My general argument here is this: that far from reproducing
contemporary "reality" Herondas pushes constantly toward a
highly aesthetic strategy of historical reference, linguistic artifact-
making, and general artistic distancing. We have arrived now at
the point where that strategy reveals itself most obviously in its
generalizing treatment of character.

The first mime is entitled "The Bawd" and turns on the axis of
Gyllis's proposition. There is something "generalizing" about that
woman's readiness to present herself in terms of her "profession"
or "role." The closer we come to her language the more clearly we
understand this readiness. When Metriche asks Gyllis why she has
so rarely come to visit, Gyllis answers in self-typifying and self-
typing language:

I live a long way off, child, and the mud in the lanes reaches up to my
knees, and my strength is as a fly's, for old age weighs me down and
the shadow stands by me. (ll. 13–16)

She makes stock language hers in such a way that she willingly
becomes, through it, a stock character. The same holds for her
comments on the Egypt into which Mandris has vanished. The
language (ll. 28–31) in which she extols the splendors of Egypt
is stock language, ancient chamber-of-commerce language. It
smothers the country in affluent generalities.

The same giving in to type is apparent in the other characters,
though they are less interesting victims of this literary process.
(Their relative simplicity may, however, help us to get closer to
the meaning of "type" in Herondas, to probe that essential notion
which I have so far only been trying to illustrate and introduce.)

Threissa has too few lines even to be a stock character, though her strategic dramatic position, between her mistress and Gyllis, is one that later comedy will incorporate into its finest strategies.

Metriche is also undeveloped. Something in her seems to represent the young, temporarily widowed woman; and from that something she acquires most of the interest she has for us. The true interest she arouses, however, centers on what I take to be, at the end of the mime, her ambiguous attitude toward Gyllis's proposition.

What does it mean to say that something "typical" is being expressed in Metriche's character, or, much more evidently, in the stock character of Gyllis? I have pointed out something of what this means in Herondas's whole literary strategy, in his peculiar literary antirealistic realism. But there is a different argument to introduce, within the more general limits of literary theory.

In what sense do Metriche or Gyllis in Mime One represent general types, in fact what does such a question mean?[5] A distinction needs to be made, before replying, between types in literature and types in life. The present question about types can only be meaningful if applied strictly to types in literature, which are far different from types in life. Types in literature are created and maintained by literature itself, while types in life—if in fact they exist—must be created and maintained by the ontological situation in which man is plunged, and out from which he reaches when he longs to create literature. Our question then is: in what sense are Metriche and Gyllis types in literature?

Gyllis is a strategic element which recurs throughout literature in a generalized form, and which serves to draw other literary characters out of themselves and toward one another. The most common form of that element is the confidante, as we see her in Euripides, Terence, or Racine. That figure is not necessarily conspiratorial; rather, as in Corneille, she tends to be only an informative factor, letting the various characters know what is being thought about them. In Racine's *Phèdre*, however, the confidante has taken a decisive turn into evil, and does what she can to destroy Hippolyte for the sake of her mistress Phèdre. Her turn toward evil is at first, characteristically, taken on behalf of her mistress, whose lust she wants to feed and satisfy. But when she realizes how deeply Phèdre's honor has been compromised she hurries to the defense, urging on Phèdre's corpse the incriminating note which leads to the destruction of Hippolyte. In this conversion we see the birth of the evil proposer, the bawd of Herondas's first Mime. I mention this genesis for a special reason.

The bawd of Mime One belongs to a subtype; to a type subordinate to the broader literary type of the confidential older woman. From one standpoint, of course, such a statement is pure pedantry. From that standpoint the bawd in Herondas is by no means a subtype; the type in question has a purely hypothetic existence; while the bawd, for all her literary heritage—in Euripides, for instance—has a very real existence, is simply what she is, in all the particularity Herondas creates into her. This argument could easily broaden into a thorough attack on the generalizing theory of the interrelations of literary works. It could turn its attack against, say, the basic assumptions of the Russian Formalists, and now the Structuralists; against those theoreticians of literature who are now, in France, contributing to literary and cultural thought so many new and arguable ideas.[6] (I think of the work of men like Lévy-Strauss or Roland Barthes, or that of the many distinguished writers for *Critique* or *Tel Quel*.) This is not the place to respond to such a broad argument; but rather the place to look at the present generalizing argument from another angle, through a different lens. In this way we get a view of the literary structure as a series of strategies at work in the service of a vision to be expressed. In dramas, those strategies involve the successful manipulation of personal forces, of *characters*, which borrow much of their nature from the experience of life-outside-literature, but which are first of all elements of artifice. In novels and epics the same fact about characters will also apply, though not as exclusively; for nowhere except in drama does the interplay of characters absorb the entire skill of the creator. Yet in novel and epic, from the viewpoint considered here, one still faces a preponderantly strategic problem of how to organize personal forces, characters, into a significant totality. (It is only that more non-character-considerations enter in these kinds than in drama; considerations of the lyrical element, the rhetorical element, and simply of a somewhat more extensive verisimilitude than is required by drama.) In drama, epic, and novel—though not in the lyric—one is thus faced with a strategic problem which must be solved, even in order to let vision, high imagination, find itself through into expression. The same exigency obviously applies to the kind of closet drama we see in Herondas's mimes.

Given this general condition of certain genres, considered as problems, it will be easier to see what the "literary type" can be and mean. We can think of such characters as Herondas's slave girl, bawd or go-between, pander, jealous woman, irascible schoolmaster, fussy old woman, naughty young schoolboy. These types were quite naturally part of the Greek literary character-baggage prior to Herondas, because they were invaluable elements in the strategy of presenting and resolving literary structures. Each of the playlets involving one of those characters, whether in Euripides, Menander, Theophrastos, or Theocritos, was faced with a basically abstract problem: how to interrelate certain forces, "spiritual" thrusts, in such a way as to create a certain spiritual effect, a minor catharsis and resolution or, to preserve the metaphor, a certain distinctive turn of energy. Character types provided, for the solution of such problems, elements like those invited by the unspecified factors in algebraic formulae; character types were ready-made elements, which could be substituted for the blank slots in the literary formula, well or badly substituted according to the skill of the author, but still in an important sense substituted, filled in. According to the prominence of the type, the magnitude or generality of its contribution to problem solving, the type becomes a major type or a subtype. To overstress *this* distinction, even from the formula viewpoint onto literature, would again be only pedantry. To call Herondas's salacious bawd a subtype of the go-between servant woman would be pedantic, unless it were clear in just what sense this distinction was being made, in an effort to see the pattern, and the prominence of the pattern, into which the character of the bawd fits. We will have plenty of chance to reconsider this kind of patterning in analyzing other mimes of Herondas. This entire discussion will keep us close to the larger argument about the distinctive distancing which marks Herondas's literary use of language; a distancing worth special attention because, though it lies deeply in his work, it may at first seem belied by his curiosity for certain details of contemporary reality.

It will finally be proper, before leaving the discussion of this mime, to say something *in context* about Herondas's meter; about

the texture of his language as music, and about the way he lodges
in it the subtle structure of his piece.

I have already said a little about the choliambic meter and its
origin. It is not a complicated prosody. The basic structure, in our
terms, is a line of six iambs of which the last is in fact not an iamb
at all, but a spondee: ⏑–/⏑–/⏑–/⏑–/– –. There are two
general and preliminary comments to make on that structure. First,
we can never think of Greek prosody precisely in our own terms,
which emphasize the alternation of stressed with unstressed syllables or feet. In ancient Greek poetry it is a question of long and
short feet, of the alternation of syllables in which the vowels take
respectively less or more time to pronounce. The basis of division
is the one familiar to us: generally between long vowels and diph-
thongs, on the one hand, and short vowels on the other hand.
This, then, is the way we must imagine the first line of the first
mime:

Thrĕíss'/ ărás/seĭ teú/ thŭrén/ tĭs; oúk/ ópséi . . .

The last foot will consist of two jammed together long, or protracted, syllables. That brings up the second preliminary comment. Ancient Greek prosody—we know this from many detailed
and extensive analyses—was extremely precise; each poet established, and on the whole seriously worked into, a ground pattern,
usually highly traditional, from which all variations were exceptionally noticeable. It is true that Herondas has built an exceptional situation, the last foot of his line, into his ground pattern,
and that he has thus somewhat domesticated the surprise element
of the last foot. Yet we must realize that this domestication was
only very limitedly possible. The choliamb was an unusual meter
to the Greeks; the more delicate and trained the ear, the more
inevitably the final foot of each line would seem to set up a small
tension with the rest of the line. Herondas was a master manipula-
tor of that tension.

III   *Mime Two*

There is no need to discuss all the extant mimes in the detail
given here to the first, for in that discussion many general matters
have been established; for example, the general character of
Herondas's prosody, his name-giving, and his concern with type-

characters. The largest trait, which comes closest to defining his whole body of work, was brought out repeatedly. I mean the distinctive posture he adopts toward the given "real" world of his own day. He seems an addict of "realism," in one sense of that term. Compared to any fifth-century writer, Herondas offers us the details of daily life; selected details of select portions of daily life, to be sure. In this he is no different from Theophrastos or Menander, to pick randomly out of the fourth century; yet even from them, I think, he distinguishes himself by his taste for the fallen world, for that part of daily life, in whose understanding he is perhaps the first ancient Greek master. Yet even in this taste, I believe, Herondas is not at all confining himself to his time or its details. His art turns on the axis of a number of temporally distancing and abstracting devices which leave us very much in doubt, finally, about how to characterize these mimes. We can say more about that later, when all the mimes have come under discussion. The issue will then be to decide to what genus these mimes belong. It will not, of course, be important to solve this matter as an exercise in classification; rather to figure out, to understand, with what kind of literature we are dealing. It will seem a useful clue, to the difficulty of the problem, that no grosser genre terms—lyric or drama, for instance—seem very useful parts of a solution to the problem.

The second mime is, I think, even more inscrutable than the first, which as we saw came to an ambiguous conclusion. Mime two, like mime eight later, is a monologue which leaves us to draw our own conclusions. The speaker is a pander, a man representing a profession for which the bawd in the first mime was an amateur representative. The pander is speaking before a court of law with a jury about an outrage perpetrated against him by a merchant-captain who does not appear in the mime.

The structure of the address is extremely simple. It opens with a pleading introduction, in which the pander Battaros contrasts his poverty to the wealth of Thales, the merchant-captain. This contrast is set against the one thing the two men have in common: that they are both foreigners, not residents of the city of Cos, where the trial is taking place. This situation argues especially against Thales's case, for he should have felt especially obligated to the laws of the city in which he was only a visitor.

At this point a clerk enters briefly—the only interruption in the

mime—to read a short, pompous clarification of the law: "When-
soever he that is free wrongeth a girl that is a slave or pursueth
her of intent, he shall pay the assessment twofold" (ll. 46–48).
Almost immediately Battaros interrupts him with a garbled am-
plification of the law, followed by a fairly direct verbal attack on
Thales. A good deal of half-learned jargon enters this attack, and
with it some quirky historical references. Then Battaros brings in
the girl, Myrtale, who allegedly had been stolen from him, and
shows her to the jury. He reminds Thales that the girl could have
been bought from him for a fair price. After a little infighting the
speech closes on a noble note, maintaining that the whole tradition of fair play and philoxenia in the city's laws is at stake in the
present trial of a foreigner. It was customary for legal cases to be
prepared, and speeches at least partially written, by hired logog-
raphers, law writers; and we can imagine that such a man must
have prepared the nobly echoing phrases and the edifying conclusion of the present talk. Yet the mixture of grandeur with vulgarity has Battaros's own stamp.

   I said that this mime is in a sense more inscrutable than the
first. Superficially, of course, the second mime is an obvious
parody, much if not all of it easily intelligible to us. Battaros is a
vulgar man exercising a profession which was always especially
contemptible to the Greeks. He is only clever enough to dress his
vulgarity in tawdrily pretentious language. He is not self-aware
enough to mute those vulgarities which most counteract his case.
Just before the clerk of court is to read the technical statement of
the law, Battaros introduces him with this:

Well, clerk, take the law of assault and read it out, and do you, good
sir, stop the hole of the water-clock till he's finished his reading lest,
as the saying goes, bladder split and bedding spoil. (ll. 41–45)

Or a little later, enriching a mere informative sentence with a
gritty proverb, he assures the gentlemen of the jury:

. . . I, gentlemen, not to bore you by long speaking and beating about
the bush, have been treated by Thales like the mouse in the pitch-pot;
I was struck with the fist. . . . (ll. 60–63)

In ways like this Herondas simply writes parody.
   How is this mime inscrutable? We start to sense the answer

when we see how the familiar literary distancing techniques oper-
ate here. Everything said about the first mime, in this regard, applies here. Of course the prosody is the same in all these pieces,
and though we can do little, from our distance in history, to make
that fact interior to us, it becomes in mimes like the second a
distinctive fact. We might otherwise suppose, for instance, that
we were dealing with a fairly direct picture, essentially a prosaic
piece of documentation, photography. We know how far from
this the truth would be. The language presented is here highly
artificial and organized under the most complex language-
historical conditions. The speech delivered by Battaros is vulgar,
but vulgar in a language-form reaching back, with every nuance
of resonance and irony, to sixth-century Ionic Greek. To realize
this is simply to appreciate again, on the elementary level, the
importance of the distancing factor.

The other ingredients of that factor are also apparent. There is
the familiar set of historical or mock-historical references. There is
the pompous mythology with which the piece closes:

Now is the hour when you will prove the might of Cos and Merops,
and the glory of Thessalos and Herakles, and the cause of Asklepios's
coming hither from Tricca and the reason wherefore Phoebe bare Leto
on this spot. (ll. 95–98)

There is the type-character creation which we noticed in the first
mime, and the exact nature of which I tried to bring a little into
the open. Battaros is a "typical pander" in a far stricter sense than
Gyllis was. Though there is tremendous originality and authenticity to his speech; though Herondas seems to have had a superb
ear for such personalities and the spice of their expressions, still
Battaros remains a type. To say that he is more "typical" than the
kind of people, in "real life," who compose his type, is true enough
and to the point here. But it is significantly misleading, in the
sense that it overstresses the relation of such literature to life; and
it minimizes the artificiality of the work. Seeing into that artificiality is seeing into the mystery of this mime.

The first mime was mysterious through a kind of innuendo
which diffused subtle evil over the entire piece. We were not allowed to get close to certain of Metriche's attitudes, and that
uncertainty was itself an ingredient in our suspicion that Metriche

was attracted by the bawd's offer. That suspicion introduced the
sense of evil, which in the bawd's proposal was too blatant to be
quite effective. The mystery of the second mime is of a different
but related kind. It rises, as in the first piece, from a tension between the realistic detail presented and the distancing literary
presentation of that detail. But in the second mime that tension is
not resolved into innuendo or irony. The mime is completely
straight-faced; the irony in it comes not from the dramatic tension
but from the external understanding which we, in subtle complic-
ity with the author, have to add to the reading of the text. We are
simply forced to experience, directly, the literary-realistic absurdi-
ties of Battaros's speech. Because of the author's careful refusal, in
this case, not to cut into the texture of his work, we are left with
the mystery of an apparent simplicity which is not in fact simple
at all.

IV *Mime Three*

I don't want to pretend that Herondas is a difficult poet in any
modern sense, or that we have to do with complex and learned
pieces of literature. The difficulty in reading Herondas comes
from another source, that we are not familiar, in any literature
contemporary or close to us, with the kind of work he offers. It
probably has its closest relatives in the moralistic character-sketch
tradition which we find in Theophrastos or La Bruyère; a tradition—as we will see more fully later—which is itself rooted in a
generic view of human nature, which is by no means modern,
which is in fact antipathetic to the widely diffused suspicion,
known to us everywhere in the literature of our century, that it is
impossible to define a human being; that finally human nature is
without determinable characteristics. This suspicion of course mil-
itates severely against the idea that men fall meaningfully into
character types. We have our own moralists—and of course all our
greatest writers are finally concerned with moral issues—but we
have a much wider and less generically defined aperture of perception onto moral questions, or onto the entire experience of human nature, than writers in previous centuries generally have had.
This is a difficulty underlying our problem in getting back to a
writer like Herondas, or Theophrastos or Menander, writers of
whom we are accustomed to say, using the term broadly, that
they were "moralists," men concerned with man's *mores,* his moral

habits of going about his life. This difficulty is one kind of reason
why we have to approach Herondas as a difficulty.

Of course there are also many specific, more precisely literary,
reasons for this difficulty, and some of these reasons have been
suggested already. I have tried to establish the point that Herondas writes as an artificer, writes away from what may at first seem
to be a tendency toward realism, in the cruder sense of the word,
as it finds itself throughout his work. This caution seemed necessary both to counteract a superficial reading of Herondas, and to
place him in terms of that historically conscious Alexandrian situation to which attention was drawn in the first chapter. The third
mime brings us face to face, however, with another kind of distancing, an artificializing factor at work in Herondas. We have
noticed it before, but with growing evidence we get more interested in its presence here. I refer to the rather gothic sado-
masochism of many of the situations arising in his work. Nowhere
in Greek literature does the pervasive historical sadness and sense
of loss, to which we referred earlier, mark itself so clearly as in
Herondas's mimes, or draw its raw material more obviously from
the subconscious areas of human experience.

The subtly insinuating flavor of the first mime can perhaps be
felt better when we read more Herondas. That Metriche contained undercurrents of unspoken response to Gyllis seems more
likely when we have grown familiar with Metrotime in mime
three. The touch of the perversely sinister in Battaros's speech—a
touch I tried to analyze above—can be felt more easily when we
have experienced the schoolmaster of the third mime. The farther
we get into this question, too, the farther we will be getting into
the meaning of "daily life" as it offers itself as a theme of Herondas's work.

The third mime opens with a protracted (ll. 1–58) speech by
Metrotime, the mother of a naughty schoolboy. Her speech is addressed to a long silent schoolmaster, who suddenly interrupts her
to say that he will do what she is asking, will punish her misbe-
having child. Then there follows a dialogue among schoolmaster,
schoolboy, and mother, in which the schoolboy begs for mercy
and promises to reform. Suddenly and surprisingly, the schoolmaster relents; at which point the disappointed mother goes off to
see "the old man," the boy's father, and to get some "footstraps" to
put on the boy.

It is worthwhile concentrating on a few of the perverse details. The introductory remarks by Metrotime are savage enough:

As you wish for any pleasure from the dear Muses, Lampriskos [the schoolmaster], and to enjoy your life, so do you beat this fellow a-shoulder, till his life [*psyche*, spirit, soul]—curse it—remain hanging on his lips. (ll. 1–4)

Herondas is ingenious at finding for his characters metaphors like the one here, which bring the intensity of their hatred very close to the surface. In many places the hatred takes a more explicitly sexual turn than it does here. After listening too long to Metrotime, Lampriskos the schoolmaster counterattacks violently against the boy, on whom, by a common perverse mechanism, he showers the hatred which he has up to this time been developing against the mother:

I'll make you more orderly than a girl—he says to Kottalos—stirring not a twig, if that's what you are after. Give me my stinging whip, the ox-tail, with which I flog the "gaol-birds" and the disgraced. Put it into my hand before I choke with choler. (ll. 66–70)

He wants to shackle and effeminize the boy, in a way almost to castrate him. Specifically, he wants to make him stationary, like an erotic ikon. The same wish-image recurs at the end of the mime. Lampriskos has there refused to punish the boy, to Metrotime's disgust. To which Metrotime answers:

On afterthought, I will go home, Lampriskos, and tell the old man of this, and return with footstraps, so that as he skips here with his feet together the Lady Muses, whom he has hated so, may witness his disgrace. (ll. 94–97)

Again, here, the image is one of impotent motion within shackles. Of course the proposed punishment, in both instances noted here, was standard for the time, as it has been until recently in our time even in Western Europe; but the turn and tone of the account here, which are what matter, are the persuasive factor. It is not hard to feel the connection between the mood of insinuation, which Gyllis expresses in mime one, and the mood of sadism established here. Gyllis is in one sense inflicting sexual punishment on Metriche by treating her as a passive sexual ikon to be placed and handled according to a plan. Gyllis and Metrotime express different neuroses; but a sick center lies between their two neuroses, and it is shared by them.

I speak of this fascination with perversity as another factor in Herondas's literary distancing.[7] Of course it is not that simple a matter, nor is it a question of deliberate strategy or of putting a literary theory into practice. Herondas writes about what interests him. In effect, though, what interests him in the present example bears directly on his relation to his past, and on the firmly traditional aspects of his literary characters.

The bridge between Herondas's interest in sado-masochistic material, and his historical-abstracting method, is his preoccupation with type character, a preoccupation which is nowhere clearer than in his exploitation of neurotic themes and *personae*. The characters onto whom he directs his most effective generic attention are those who, like Gyllis, Battaros, or Metrotime, most represent a kind of frozen and neurotic behavior. It is well-known, as a fact of life if only that, that neurotic behavior is above all frozen and rigid; and this fact of psychology allows itself, in Herondas's work, to be translated quite directly into the practice of his literary skill. Type characters in Herondas—and perhaps in general—are in this sense peculiar abstractions from the suppleness of human existence.

It should be added, about the third mime, that there is a better chance in it, than in the first two mimes, to see the artifice and artistry of Herondas at work in a broadly literary way. We have again the same raw material: the brilliant but teasing choliambs. Built into that material, we have the same tense structure of personal relations. But the whole picture is more complex and revealing this time.

There is always an intently listening second or third party in these mimes. In the first mime we are made keenly aware of the listening, little speaking, psyche of Metriche, as well as of the almost entirely mute Threissa. Metriche reacts, we know, to every insinuation of Gyllis. Her unspoken reactions constitute the center of the piece; Herondas is that skillful at manipulating silence. In the second mime, we have effectively only one speaker; the reader is the audience of the speech of Battaros. The silence in which we listen to Battaros has something in common with that silence in which Metriche listens to Gyllis in the first mime. We add much of the tenseness to the second mime with our attention. The third mime works out its tensions in a genuine drama, of which Herondas is the master.

The character of that drama, as we saw above, is extremely simple. The mother speaks at length to characters of whom we have as yet no concrete experience. We are simply waiting for the tirade, for the shapes of addressed characters to emerge. We are held off, properly, until many details have whetted our appetites: we have learned how the boy can't read, though "his knuckle-bones lie far glossier than our oil-flask"; that "if we even raise our voices in rebuke, either for three days he refuses to visit the threshold of our house, and eats his grandmamma, an old lady, destitute of livelihood, out of house and home, or else sits on the top of the roof, stretching his legs apart and peering down like some monkey" (ll. 36–41); and so on. It comes as a felicitous shock when the schoolmaster bursts in with: "Metrotime, you may spare your imprecations." The shock is the more felicitous because this brief interruption picks up in the middle of the previous line, carrying that unfinished line to its perfect metrical conclusion. (It is like the stichomythy, in Greek tragedy, which involves one character picking up and finishing another's line.)

The schoolmaster's imprecation is rapidly heightened; he goes beyond Metrotime and asks at once for "his stinging whip." We are startled and attentive. We still have no direct experience of the boy. When the boy comes we are again surprised; these mimes are so brief and fast-paced that we are constantly kept on the alert, and never certain what is coming. It is Herondas's great strength that he manipulates this strategic advantage perfectly, never abusing it, always using it fully. This time, it seems, we see both terror and humor. The boy is beside himself with fear, and we can feel this as though we were inside him; at the same time, though, he is almost a comic caricature, so much the type of the caught and threatened bad schoolboy that we laugh at how perfectly he fulfills our expectations.

Nay, nay, I beseech you, Lampriskos, by the Muses, and by your beard and by your poor little Kottalos's life, don't flog me with the stinger, but with the other one. (ll. 71–73)

The "other one" may be a softer strap or a reed. The off-handed-ness of such phrases, in Herondas, forever keeps his text close to speech, and provides it with what is most remarkably "realistic" in his whole body of work.

There follows an interplay, between schoolmaster and boy, which is a verbal ballet of threats and prayers, and which carries the whole drama to a kind of pointillistic excitement. That excite-ment is broken only—and this is the most unexpected turn of all—by the schoolmaster's sudden relenting. Metrotime is angry at this relenting, but not as astounded as we feel she would naturally be; perhaps her fury had previously been frustrated in this way. We are finally surprised by the resigned-sadistic tone with which she announces her next move: to go home for the footstraps.

On that tone the mime ends, noncommittally, a little puzzlingly, like all Herondas's pieces. At the end of the first mime we were unsure of Metriche's attitude; at the end of the second we were unsure how to feel toward Battaros. In both cases Herondas was concealing his own position within the mime. That is what hap-pens in the third, too. The sadism incarnated here is kept intact, as end tone and final resonance, by the mother's last words, about the Muses and the footstraps. The artistry of that conclusion re-flects itself throughout this dramatic piece, and does so more obvi-ously than in the simpler structure of the first two mimes. The entire third piece is a play of tensions among three people whose words are only gradually released into the action; and the conclu-sion of the mime keeps the tension in all those tensions. At the end the mother is simply starting the theme of the mime all over again. Compared to this the first two mimes end where they end.

With the third mime, more clearly than with the first two, it is relevant to say something fresh about the sense in which Heron-das is not in any easy way a "realist." I have up to now made that point largely in terms of his complex traditionalism, his stance within Greek literary history. But I have also been stressing his interest in the generic, as in his creation of character-types, and the way in which that interest grew out of a withdrawal from the unresolved detail of experience. (That withdrawal had seemed to be a conscious simplification of reality, which has been perhaps the favored exit of realistic writers at all times, from immersion in the undifferentiated presence of being; from the kind of immersion which Joyce, for instance, seemed willing to face and Zola did not.) That interest is related to the strategic operation of the third, and of several other of Herondas's mimes. For in the third mime Herondas works with dramatic tensions as he works with type characters. He builds up lines of force, and patterns of action and reaction, in establishing his tension, which are finally elements of *structural* mastery; and the structural concern revealed there is nowhere else so clearly visible, in Herondas, as in the attention he pays to types of character which satisfy the exigencies of his dramatic argument.

V *Mime Four*

The analysis of Herondas's art should enrich itself as we move from one mime to the next. So should our awareness of the techniques we are using for analysis. At the end of the previous section, for example, it became clear that we were moving closer to the possibilities of a structural analysis; for instance toward the kind of analysis carried out on tales from Boccaccio by Tzvetan Todorov in his *Grammaire du Décaméron*,[8] or already by the Russian formalist critics in the second decade of this century. We were turning to the essential patterns of movement within the mime; and we will later be able to look back over Herondas's entire achievement in terms of this kind of criticism. We had previously looked into other ways in which Herondas withdrew from direct presentation of the reality of his day. He stylized his experience of that reality by dealing it out in character types, by placing those types in somewhat formulated tales, and by embedding the entire effort in language which both in meanings and prosody leaned toward the previous history of the Greek language and the culture borne forward by it. Becoming more aware of the critical approaches, by which we neared Herondas's work, in all these cases meant becoming aware of the work itself. Each mime added to the discussion has meant an increase in this process of awareness and understanding. With each addition we have reexperienced the intricate interweaving of criticism with actual understanding, of the theoretical assumption with the nature of the practical discovery.

A reading of the fourth mime adds a great deal to what we have found so far. Though it is still domestic comedy, still a study of men (or women) and their manners, it involves both real things and "real" contemporary relations to them, in a way not nearly so obvious in the earlier pieces. So far we have been in a living room, a law court, and a schoolhouse (or so it seemed); yet though the action has been local and contemporary, the actual physical settings have been general and generalized, like the largely typed characters who have been placed in those settings.

In this mime we are with two women, Kynno (the mistress) and Kokkale (her ingénue servant), at dawn, at a temple of Asclepios, probably the large Asclepieion of Kos, which was excavated between 1902 and 1904. At first the two women are simply waiting for the temple to open. Kynno begins with an elaborate prayer, which, as we know from an inscription, is close to the formulae actually used at an Asclepieion. (Though we can hardly know an ancient language well enough to know at just what small points variations are introduced, and irony brought along with those variations. And this ignorance, on our part, is precisely the most frustrating one; for in the present case, by way of example, we soon find out in other ways that Kynno is pretentious and ill-informed in her talking with Kokkale.) The maidservant is amazed and astonished by the art-works in the temple:

La: Kynno dear, what beautiful statues: What craftsman was it who worked this stone, and who dedicated it? (ll. 21–23)

She is predictably fascinated by exaggerated realism:

See, dear,—she blurts out to Kynno—the girl yonder looking up at the apple; wouldn't you think she will swoon away suddenly, if she does not get it? Oh, and yon old man, Kynno. Ah, in the Fates's name, see how the boy is strangling the goose. Why, one would say the sculpture would talk, that is if it were not stone when one gets close. (ll. 26–33)

It seems almost as though Herondas is parodying the realistic attitude with which he himself flirts, then finally rejects.

Later Kokkale speaks of a naked boy, who "will bleed, will he not, if I scratch him . . . for the flesh seems to pulse warmly as it lies on him in the picture . . ." (ll. 59–62). This kind of confusion between art and "reality" is a commonplace of Greek aesthetic thought and of all later, Greek-influenced thought, as well. The grapes which Apelles painted, and which the blackbirds tried to eat off the painting, were a stock illustration for this thought, and were pulled out by subtle minds like Plato's when they wanted to characterize the basic intention of plastic art; and much of Plato's criticism of art, for that matter, was directed against what he considered art's misguided effort simply to reproduce reality, instead of re-presenting it. Herondas not only takes us into that tradition here but, I believe, introduces into it, through Kokkale, not only an ironic but a new, erotic, note. The way in which Kokkale speaks of the naked boy in the last passage cited makes us appreciate a new weakness and flaw in the reproduction view of art: that it takes the life out of the object of art, and out of the art-object, by making it static and fleshy. Herondas's concern with the erotic helps him to make this point here.

Therefore, in quite an intellectual, and at the same time comical, spirit Herondas introduces us in this mime to some of the "real" things in his culture. (This is another way to describe what "realism" means for Herondas.) The entire piece is an example, perhaps as striking as any we can find in Greek literature, of attention to the actual, concrete mood of ancient Hellenic social life: we hear real voices, see real faces, touch real things; if ever we want to use the word *real* in its most ordinary sense, and to insist on that usage, it is here. It seems the kind of literary work from which one could write a chapter in sociology. Yet, to repeat this theme again, it seems to me even more interesting to discuss again the senses in which this work is intensely literary, and in fact very little concerned with making itself a record of social behavior. Perhaps something in the work's realism forces a reaction against that realism, which counters the character of anything in language. But I think my response, in this case, is not simply a reaction.

The language, stock attitudes, and stock interrelationships of the two women, in the fourth mime, all go to stylize the work. It is especially interesting to see how that stylization draws up, into itself, the real material which is being presented, the hard objects in the temple and the flesh-and-blood people outside it. Everything experienced here is rapidly drawn up into the consciousness of the perceiver, so that even the hard realistic statues are made peculiarly a function of the person—in this case, of the naïve, wondering person—for whom they are of interest. This perceiving takes place in the resonant, and highly literary, prosody to which

I continually refer here; from which all traces of ordinary conversation have been purged, so that one never feels, when "seeing choliambically" through the eyes of Kokkale, that he is seeing with the eyes of everyday life. It is finally of special interest, in defining the character of a mime like this, that the two women speak off against each other almost as in an operatic recital. Kokkale acts as straight man, or woman, forever asking leading questions about what they are seeing, and Kynno gladly fills up the huge holes left by Kokkale's questions. The stylization of this device is enhanced by a passage in which Kynno addresses a slave girl who is not present in the dialogue of the text. Kynno addresses her this way:

Kydilla, go and call the sacristan. It's you I am speaking to, you who are gaping up and down! La! not an atom of notice does she take of what I am saying, but stands and stares at me for all the world like a crab! Go, I tell you again, and call the sacristan. You glutton, there is not a patch of ground, holy or profane, that would praise you as an honest girl—everywhere alike your value is the same. Kydilla, I call this god to witness, that you are setting my wrath aflame, little as I wish my passion to rise. I repeat, I call him to witness that the day will come when you shall have cause to scratch your filthy noodle. (ll. 41–51)

This subaddress, to a figure who does not appear in the closet drama, is organically and masterfully handled. It is handled in such a way that the formalization of attitudes, among the main characters, is emphasized; the formalization which results from what is essentially an extended aside. My secondary point, in citing this passage, brings us back again to our discussion of the third mime, to the sado-masochistic material which was turned up there. The master-slave, master-servant, master-schoolboy relationship seems generally to set off or trigger that tone in Herondas. This point is here of literary, not of psychoanalytical, interest; it helps us to see once again, in the present context, how operatically Herondas weaves together the personalities who make up the whole person, we might say the whole answering face of himself, which his entire work creates.

VI *Mime Five*

The present argument keeps diffracting and then reforming itself; I think this is the most valuable strategy in the criticism of literature. We can hardly hope to make conclusive statements about anything as indeterminate, subtle, and self-transforming as the projection (and concealing) of a whole human personality in the traditional matter of literature. We have to keep trying, then begin over again. In a small way that is what I attempt to do in beginning over with the discussion of each new mime.

There are many ways in which these pieces assert their own self-conscious artistry. They simulate the direct "expression of reality" while at all times pulling back from that simulation. Their ways of pulling back are various: by language, through traditionalist prosody and verbal resonance; by character portrayal, through the strategy of type-creation, and stylization of all which is most individual; psychologically, through those infusions of neurosis by which Herondas contrives to free his characters from the norms of daily life which we customarily associate with realism. A very considerable artistry holds together these distancing strategies, and of course finally confers on them not only their immunity to any banal reasoning but their gift for raising ordinary life to new forms.

The fifth mime raises familiar points again, most of them in just the way they were raised in mime three. But the differences are instructive and help us to appreciate especially the sado-masochistic material which Herondas works into his literary world. It will be useful, once more, to remember the distinction between psychology in the "real world," and the use of the experience of psychology in literature. This distinction is a subtle and evanescent one, hard to analyze and hard to hold, as is the difference between literature and life. But it is a firm distinction in its subtlety. It needs a subtle hand to hold it.

This time the schoolmaster is replaced by a jealous woman, Bitinna, and the naughty schoolboy is replaced by a slave who has been off whoring; his name is Gastron. This time, though, there is an interceder, Bitinna's daughter Kydilla, who begs for mercy for Gastron.

These differences play themselves off against the same background of interweaving emotions, hostility, jealousy, fear, and release at the end, which was at work in the third mime; and, at least to the student of Herondas, it is this counterpoint with the earlier mime which is peculiarly interesting here.

We approach closer to a genuine drama, or playlet, in mime five

than anywhere else in Herondas, and for the future development
of literary history it is this, more than anything else, which draws
our attention to the present piece. At first the jealous slave-owner
simply berates Gastron:

Tell me, Gastron [a name which plays on the word belly, *gaster*], have
you waxed so fat, that my legs are not enough for your sport, but you
must press your suit with Amphytale wife of Menon. (ll. 1–3)

Then she slides into the expected menace:

Bind this fellow—what? not started yet?—loose the rope of the bucket
quickly and bind him. If I don't disgrace you and make you an example to the whole place, count me no woman. . . . Come, you, by your-
self, strip him of his cloak and bind him. (ll. 10–18)

Gastron puts in:

Nay, nay, Bitinna, I beseech you by your knees. (l. 19)

Bitinna:

Strip him, I repeat. You must know that you are a slave, and that I
paid three minas for you. Oh! ill betide that day which first brought
you here. Pyrrhies, you'll pay for this; that's nothing like binding him.
Pinion his elbows behind him, and let the rope cut into his flesh.
(ll. 20–25)

To this the slave replies, with a plea for compassion which almost
touches us, though at the same time we know it is the eternal plea
of the irremediable slave, of that Davus of Roman comedy, who
always, obstreperously and impudently, invites misery onto himself, then always begs for mercy. This is the stock scalliwag
character in ancient literature, who most mixes our feelings of
contempt and compassion; here his call for compassion is a cry toward our own compassion.

The dark figure of Pyrrhies plays an almost silent part in the
remainder of the mime. (He reminds us of the abused slave
Kydilla in mime four; and of other slaves soon to be seen: and he
makes us aware how clearly Herondas is addressing us on the
matter of the situation of the slave.) Soon he is criss-crossing the

background of the play, carrying out the demands of Bitinna. At
the same time Bitinna is beginning to weaken, although we can
only very slowly see in through the chinks of her armor. We listen
with great attention at this point. Gastron asks:

Are you going to kill me, Bitinna, without proving first whether the
charge is true or false? (ll. 35–36)

And she says:

What about the words you said just now with your own tongue,
"Bitinna, forgive me this error"? (ll. 37–38)

The way she says this puts us on guard. She is probing to learn
what he meant, probably also hoping in the back of her mind to
convince herself that he is still true to her. But he does not quite
satisfy her desire to delude herself:

I was only wanting to cool your passion. (l. 39)

he says. That is too much for her in her nervous state. She turns to
Pyrrhies and, of course, takes out her anger first on him by the
kind of psychic turn which, in the previous mime, led the mother
to turn her anger from her son to the schoolmaster:

Are you still standing there looking on and not taking him where I tell
you? Kydilla, hit this villain on the beak, and you, Drechon, go with
him at once wherever he leads the way. Girl, give this cursed fellow a
rag to hide his damned tail . . . that he may not be seen going
through the market-place naked. (ll. 40–46)

Gastron is carted off by his fellow slave Pyrrhies, and for a moment we think the little drama is over and will have to end. But
there are two more touches. Bitinna calls Pyrrhies back, saying:

tell Kosis the tattooer to come with needles and ink. . . . Let him be
hung up as bemummed as his honour Davus. (ll. 65–68)

At this point Kydilla intervenes with a plea for compassion which
is of considerable literary historical interest.

No, mama, this time, as you hope that your Batyllis may live, and that
you may see her married, and lift her children in your arms, this time
let him go; this one error, I beseech you. (ll. 69–73)

Bitinna is at first outraged.

Am I to let go this double-dyed slave? (ll. 74–75)

But by now we have learned how to listen between Bitinna's lines.
We have seen the fragile foundation, of hope, of jealousy, and
personal pain, on which her sadism is based; and we no longer
have much confidence in her power to hold onto a single emotion.
Herondas has managed to reveal so much in so short a time. Even
granting the distinction between psychology in life and psychology in art we must admit that he seems, in many of these mimes,
to be bringing the fruit of accurate and perceptive experience of
"abnormal psychology" in life. The poem ends appropriately, and
beautifully, with the working out of this weakness of Bitinna. She
gives in to the force of the whole situation, and to the last pressure
of it, Kydilla's plea for mercy:

But it is the twentieth, and only four days to the Gerenia. (l. 80)

Headlam's long note on this line reminds us how greatly we are
indebted to scholarship for understanding even relatively clear
and open ancient texts, like that of Herondas. He assembles a lot
of evidence for the fact that in the days immediately preceding
and following sacred festivals it was forbidden, in Athens, to punish prisoners or slaves. (The most famous example is the post-
ponement of the death of Socrates until the sacred ship could return from Delphi; because during the absence of the ship the city
was in a state of ritual purity.) The point is all that is needed to
give Bitinna the way out she needs. For as her frenzy of imagined
punishments grows more intense, we grow less convinced that she
will carry through. The threat of tattooing seems, in this mime, as
unfirm as the threat of leg-irons in the schoolmaster mime. She
gives in at last:

Well, I will let you go for this time, and you must be duly grateful to
this girl, whom I brought up in my arms and love as well as Batyllis;

but when we have poured our drink-offerings to those that sleep, there
will be no honey then in the feast *you* will keep day after day. (ll.
81–85)

The last clause is her last gasp of self-respect; all else is gone. The
eighty-five-line poem ends as perfectly as a small symphony. It is
complete and brief.

I mentioned above the reason for looking rather closely at the
present mime. It is a more ambitious literary whole than are the
first four mimes, though the fifth is very much a piece with its
predecessors. It is more ambitious because it both raises and
solves a literary problem more fully than the earlier mimes. The
simplest of those was probably the second, the pander-mime; the
most complex was probably the third, the schoolmaster-mime: the
difference between the fifth and the third is perhaps a fine one,
but through it we can locate some of the new possibilities which
begin to open in Herondas's work.

In the present mime new sources of compassion provide, in a
happy and most instructive way, the key to technical advance. In
the third mime Metrotime never relents. At the end she is going
off to ask for leg-irons with which to fetter the boy. Only the
schoolmaster has relented, but not in a way that suggests he even
cares greatly about punishing Lampriskos. In the fifth mime,
however, Bitinna genuinely relents, at the urging of Kydilla, it is
true, but nonetheless genuinely. It is not a great scene of relenting. There is, as always in the attitude of Herondas, the manipula-
tor toward his poems, a distinct irony and even cynicism about
any finer emotions he elicits from his characters. (About the art-
love of Kokkale in Mime Four; about the schoolmaster's relenting,
in Mime Three; about the pander's upright rhetoric in mime two;
about the surface righteousness of Metriche, in Mime One.)
Bitinna and Gastron in no way remind us of Achilles and Priam;
the comparison is in every way laughable and intended to be, if in
fact Herondas at all heard such echoes when he worked in a form
like the present one. Yet in a modest way we do have here a scene
of relenting which answers Gastron's plea for compassion.

That relenting enables Herondas to conclude the present mime;
in a sense he had not concluded, but simply brought to an end,
the first four mimes. Viewing those mimes merely as vignettes it is
possible, of course, to consider them "closed"; and in literary-

historical fact, of course, they were closed, concluded; we have them in their entirety and there is nothing missing. In any deeper sense, though, they simply come to an end. They are snapshots or, better, short documentaries. The fifth mime is an exception.

Relenting, here quite as much as in the *Iliad*, at the end of the *Oresteia*, or in *Oedipus at Colonus* (where the gods relent), makes a literary conclusion possible. It makes resolution possible, which is a kind of literary solution. I dare say, though, that we are not faced here with an entirely literary issue. We are faced with a human situation on which literature can draw, but the dominant tone and characteristics of which literature can never dictate. That human situation provides terms for literary-technical solution, which might otherwise be undiscoverable. We are led by seeing this to see an important kind of bond between mortality— taken in a very wide sense—and literary technique. Where mortality means, as in the present example, a mature sense of human possibility, of human growth in grace or in mere humaneness, a technical solution may be less hard to find for the problem of presenting and fulfilling the text which embodies that human situation. This is still a qualified point. But it is one worth developing, and we will add to the repertoire of topics under consideration here, as we move toward a more comprehensive view of Herondas's achievement.

VII *Mime Six*

There are many arguments at work here, too many to take stock of at regular intervals. It would be tedious and useless to summarize all the issues as we go along: to summarize the character of Herondas's language, the nature of his characterizations, the peculiar traits of his prosody, the psychological intricacies of his work. We are perhaps overdue, however, on one of these issues; and the fifth mime forces it back onto us again.

I am thinking of Herondas's use of stock-characters. In the present argument, the topic of "psychological intricacies" has for a while replaced that of stock-characters; but in fact the two themes are tightly interrelated. The relation of schoolmaster to mother to schoolboy, in Mime Three, or that of mistress to slave in Mime Five, is a stock relationship which draws characters up into "stockness." That is, we come here on at least a fresh way of looking into the question of the stock character.

The third and fifth mimes both turn on the sadistic relationship of an angry female to a recalcitrant but contrite younger man (son or slave); and on intercession—from schoolmaster or servant girl—which frees the expectant victim. The roles played by the three interrelated figures, in these two mimes, impose fairly specific characteristics on them. The aggressive, beseeching, and intermediary character traits, which are mobilized by these situations, are highly generalized, as though they were to fit into the opening of an algebraic formula. Formulaic situation fosters and flows from a rather abstract level of characterization. This is another and important way to think about the question of character types, and though we have discussed the matter earlier, the reading of mimes three and five helps us come closer to it.

The sixth mime draws us away from this immediate issue, though not far away. It returns us to the world of, say, the first mime, to a mild but sinister domestic environment. Yet in its way it reminds us of the character-type and situation-type issues. We will see at once what form this takes.

The story is extremely simple, though it contains innuendoes of female psychology, which are very subtle, and a great many nuances of language which contribute vastly to the effect of the whole piece. The title is well translated as "A Friendly Chat." Koritto is entertaining her friend Metro in her house; but that entertaining is, in its way, harsh from the beginning. Just after inviting Metro to sit down, Koritto turns to her slave girl, against whom she delivers a bitter—but by now quite familiar—tirade:

Be grateful to my guest here, but for whose presence I'd have given you a sound taste of my hands. (ll. 10–11)

Metro tries to draw Koritto back to the subject of the visit, though it is difficult. At last she succeeds, and gets out her question:

Please tell me the truth, dear Koritto, who stitched you the scarlet baubon? (ll. 17–19)

(A *baubon* was a leather replica of a phallos.) Koritto asks how Metro knows of the baubon. Koritto is furious when she learns that the object, which she had loaned to Eubule, wife of Bitas, has been passed on to Nosis, Erinna's daughter, and that Metro had

seen it with Nosis. Koritto hated Nosis before but now loathes her.
Metro tries the role of counsellor, advising Koritto that

A pious woman should endure all things . . . (l. 39)

After a little cajoling Koritto reveals that Kerdon stitched the
baubon. There follows a long discussion between the two women
about which of three Kerdons is in question. (This whole gossipy
sub-theme is delightfully handled.) Koritto soon settles the discussion with a panegyric on the workmanship of the true Kerdon.
His baubons are

firmer than the real article, and not only that, but as soft as sleep, and
the laces are more like wool than leather . . . ; a kinder cobbler to a
woman you could not possibly find. (ll. 69–73)

The topic is so lovely and compelling that Koritto momentarily
forgets her hatred of Nosis and Eubule. Metro asks Koritto why
she didn't also bring a certain second baubon from Kerdon, and
learns that Koritto had been accompanied by another woman and
felt it tactless to ask for more, though she had been so tempted
that she had considered granting "the last favors" to Kerdon.
Shortly afterwards Metro declares that she must soon go to
"Artemis, wife of Kandas the tanner, . . . to find out all about
Kerdon." She closes her remarks, however, with the disarming
middle-class finale:

Farewell, sweet Koritto; my old man is hungry and it's time to be making my way home. (ll. 97–98)

We realize at once, as we did with Metriche in the first mime, that
we are dealing with an orthodox middle-class woman; neither
with a sex maniac nor with a whore. (One thinks of the newspa-
per reports, familiar enough in our daily press, of prostitution and
bed-swapping in the lives of suburban middle-class American
housewives.) Koritto echoes her guest's prudence in the aphoristic
close of the piece:

Shut the door, you there, hen-girl, and count to see whether the hens
are all safe, and throw them some darnel. For it's a fact that the bird-

fanciers will rob one, even if one keeps them in one's lap. (ll. 98–102)

This is another slap at a slave. The evidence on this point is cumulative and telling. We have more proverbial language and thought. Above all, though, we have another brusque move back from the world of erotic self-gratification into the world of prudence and middle-class caution. That is part of the piquancy of Herondas. But there is even more artistry working at this point, which Herondas carefully turns back into the whole mime. Hen-snatching recalls baubon-snatching; Koritto is still thinking of her perfidious friend Eubule, who loaned Koritto's scarlet baubon to Nosis.

The literary strategy employed here is somewhat more complex than that of the first mime, where innuendo also tended to take over the function of strategy. The conflict between erotic desire and bourgeois comfort, with its attendant implied values, is here brought very clearly to the surface, in a way which illustrates the strategy in many of the earlier mimes, and helps us to see, in them, another way in which they conceal character-type and type-situations.

It is obvious, but not too obvious to restate and restudy, that the starting point in Herondas is a bourgeois world, in a sense in which nothing similar existed or at least let itself be portrayed in earlier Greek literature, though we do find the same world in Menander and Theophrastos. In the Introduction and first chapter of this book I gave considerable attention to some of the changes between earlier Greek culture and literature and that world—especially the Alexandrian world—which by definition existed at least partially as a looking-back to the earlier. I spoke of a certain sadness in the retrospection with which the later world existed in terms of the earlier, and I still think that perspective applies, say, in the case of Herondas.[9] His way of avoiding the realism, which he seems to promise, is to artificialize his presentation of the world; and this he seems especially to accomplish by prosody, vocabulary, and stylizations of character which reveal his literary nostalgia. However, his concern with the "bourgeois" reality of his own day is a form of historical nostalgia, which is somewhat different from any stressed here so far.

Nostalgia may at first seem to be a curious word to describe

Herondas's portrayal of bourgeois life. (Earlier we talked about sadness, a related notion). We need to look very closely at the society with which he does seem preoccupied. As he shows it, that society is highly stylized, and if we call it bourgeois we need to realize that it is distanced from actuality far more than—to pick a startling contrast—the social portrayals in Zola's *Germinal* or James Gould Cozzens's *By Love Possessed* were distanced from the societies they portrayed. Characters, their values, and the social values "behind" those personal values lie at the center of the six mimes studied so far. The bawd, the pander, the schoolmaster, the two women offering in the temple, the jealous woman, the women discussing the baubon; all these figures are types expressing values which we find prominent in societies where a middle class has taken over.

It is wrong to speak of middle-class society in the modern, post-Renaissance sense, and to expect it to apply satisfactorily to the society of any sector of the ancient world. Loosely speaking, though, certain traits are the same in those two periods, in ours and in that of Hellenistic Greece. Money comes more widely into circulation than before, and introduces with it a new social mobility. New wealth is accumulated, and in consequence new classes; most prominently a new aristocracy of wealth, including the nouveaux riches, which replaces the aristocracy of birth. New character types are thrown up by this total situation, and new relationships among those characters. Caution, prudence, inhibition, prurience, taste for obscenity: it is a too general, but on the whole sadly accurate, fact that these traits become trademarks of bourgeois society.

These very broad and shallow observations may at least help us to look freshly at the world shown in Herondas's mimes, and through them, to look at least fleetingly at the actual world of that time. We can be sure this world lies somewhere on the far side of those mimes, somehow unclear, through a diffracted glass, but actual and somehow a guarantee of the work portraying them. We had already approached the question in discussing Mime Six, the conclusion of which seemed to return us so fliply into a world of middle-class values. The question of the nature and authenticity of that world, as permanent background, is raised by all these mimes. They tend, as I have said, to be set in interiors, in living rooms, law courts, temples and temple compounds, cobblers' shops, which enclose them into the intimacy of middle-class society. They deal with those intimacies, of social intercourse, social awe, and social pleading, which by contrast with the world of tragic values, or that of Greek speculative thought, seem narrow and—according to one's perspective, of course—all too human. Finally they deal with those small resolutions, of tone, manner, and outcome, which are far fallen from the codas of high Greek drama.

All this we can safely affirm of Herondas, as of Theophrastos, Menander, and the Aristotle of the *Ethics*. I will attempt to make those connections clearer in the next chapter; as well as to elaborate on some of those traits which mark Herondas off as part of his age, as an Alexandrian. At this point though I want to restate, and rephrase, my general argument about the artificializing operation, which Herondas performs on the description of his contemporary "bourgeois" society.

So far we have made no effort to probe deeply into the relation of poet to society. Undoubtedly, most of the discussion so far has turned on the vocabulary and assumptions of an Aristotelian mimetic theory; of an aesthetic for which the artwork would in some reliable sense be an "imitation" or "representation" of a world perceived out-there. The coercion of this dualistic assumption is very strong. It has its philosophical roots in the dualism of eighteenth-century epistemologists, like Locke and Hume, who have continually dominated at least the Anglo-Saxon intellectual world, while their French contemporaries, like Condillac, La Mettrie, and Diderot beguiled the Continent. But the Aristotelian aesthetic has other, related but even more tenacious, roots in the linguistic habits by which we discuss and describe the work of artistic creators. Our preoccupation with content, as the center of art-works, may be the clue to our problem. We naturally think of the art-work as being "about" something, or some things, in the outer world. We are ill at ease in talking about form, whether it is surface form like rhyme, or what the German critic Oskar Walzel called "inner form," the organic striving for shape which takes place from the inside of the work out.[10]

These inherited assumptions, for which I can give only a shorthand explanation here, certainly coerce our language of aesthetics, and make it difficult for us to realize freshly what goes on in the artistic transaction. To realize that requires always a certain limited taste for literary psychoanalysis; and to indulge such a taste always involves a great danger, especially when we are directing attention to a writer who lived long ago, and about whom we have almost no hard information. We have to move in the dark. Yet there are some general directions in that darkness, and we should make what use of them we can.

We know that any author's, any man's, apprehension of the nature of his society develops both very slowly and from the earliest period of his life. It is only gradually that a man realizes he lives "in a society." When he begins to enter that realization he only gradually knows what, in the broadest sense, to call his society, how to make it a conscious whole in his mind. This gradual development is in a real sense without end. A man's society becomes a universe of apprehension, of more or less clear awareness, inside him; and because that awareness is huge and internal he can never completely encompass it. It is quite unrealistic to imagine that a man—whether an Alexandrian Greek, twentieth-century American, or an Ibo bard—can imitate, or represent his society, even in the broadest interpretation of that Aristotelian phrase. Man, either as human being generally or artist specifically, lives inside his society more than such an Aristotelian perspective would make intelligible.

All this helps *in a general way* with the analysis of Herondas. Even that general usefulness is valuable to us here. For when we notice, say, the new bourgeois world appearing in the character types and character situations of Herondas's mimes, we are at first tempted to imagine that he is looking at, and then portraying, what "he sees outspread before him." This temptation is dangerous, for it leads back into the antiliterary, time-bound critical prejudices which I have been trying to counteract throughout the argument here. This temptation leads into the view of Herondas as "portraying his time."

I think it is important to find the correct critical language here. Herondas is in fact internalizing the experience of his time, is proving in his work that his time existed for him primarily as language. When we see this we grow readier, from a fresh angle, to understand the main argument being made here, that Herondas is above all an artist carrying on a dialogue with his own literary tradition. We will specifically appreciate more clearly that in his "portrayal" of the bourgeois, which was in fact becoming the dominant social class of his time, he was really working out his own microcosm of character types and character-type situations. This brings us back into the center of our entire argument.

VIII   *Mime Seven*

It brings us very neatly up to the seventh mime; and this mime enables us to carry the present argument farther. We come now to a piece which seems almost a baroque elaboration on the preceding, almost a dwelling on all the possibilities of the cobbler scene.

On the surface there is very little to recount. Metro brings people to Kerdon:

Kerdon, I am bringing you these ladies to see whether you have any cunning handiwork worth showing them. (ll. 1–3)

Kerdon responds gratefully, though with a certain characteristic harshness. He attacks a slave for not attending properly to his work.

Drimylos, it is you I am talking to! What? Asleep again? Pistos, beat him on the nose, till he sheds off all his sleeping fit. Nay, rather on his spine. . . . (ll. 5–8)

Then Kerdon opens out his displays of elegant shoes, sprinkling his professional shoe-language with angry explosions against Pistos, the second of his two helpers. The wares are praised in language which reminds us of the admiring language of the ladies in the temple (fourth mime). The cobbler prattles endlessly about his shoes and slaves. There is an extraordinary mock-epic list of shoes:

. . . here are all kinds, Sicyonian, Ambraciot, Nossis-shoes, Chian, parrots, hempen, saffron shoes, common shoes, Ionian button-boots, "night hoppers," "ankle-tops," red shoes, Argive sandals, scarlet, "youths," "steps." . . . (ll. 56–61)

When Kerdon is questioned about the price of a particular pair, he answers in a tone so brutal and patronizing, at the same time, that we are reminded of the legalistic pander of Mime Two. He has the pander's same rude unconscious gift for making himself disgusting. He is the kind of person who will speak of "this gray head on which the mange has settled." Simultaneously, he conceals the price of the items about which he is being questioned. To which he adds, in a kind of aside to himself:

. . . you will admit, if truth you will say, that you should not lightly dismiss any handiwork of cobblers . . . truly if my cast doesn't catch something now I don't know how I shall keep my pot boiling. . . . (ll. 69–71, 75–76)

Headlam's introduction to the mime suggests at least two innuendos of this whole argument, which are not immediately apparent. Mangy or even bald heads were on the whole both laughable and disgusting in ancient Greece. Bald people were usually "parasites, *lenones* [pimps], and braggarts." [11] But there is more to it, and Headlam reminds us, even in connection with a passage like the present one, that more is at work here; for cobblers were in fact centers of intrigue and gossip, and their shops were centers of distribution of objects like the baubon of Mime Six, which were favored by wealthy ladies with time on their hands.

At that point one of the ladies blames Kerdon for not stating explicitly what his prices are. A little haggling takes place, until Metro addresses Kerdon, asking him what he would charge a certain lady for a certain pair of shoes. To this he replies, in a sudden and grotesque rush of gallantry, that if she, Metro, were to request the shoes he would give them to her for nothing. For others he would do nothing of the sort; only for her. In the brilliant concluding lines, which consist of Kerdon's muttered shoptalk, and of asides to different people standing around the room, he never forgets Metro. In his concluding words, full of innuendo, he says:

But do you, Metro, mind and come back to me on the ninth to get some red slippers; for the wise must stitch his cloak indoors out of the heat. (ll. 128–29)

Most of what I have said of the earlier mimes could be repeated here, and could be taken to support the general argument. The sinister, almost gothic atmosphere of the piece draws attention back away from its "realism." The characters, especially Kerdon, are typecast, and their relations to one another are stereotyped.

The language employed is the same artificializing choliambic, surrounding the same semi-archaizing vocabulary. All of the reasons I
gave earlier for not considering this literature realistic could be
repeated here.

It is obvious that I have been working toward just this point,
about "realism." But it is equally obvious that "realism" means
many different things, and that in its cruder and more program-
matic forms it does not have now and has probably never had,
many proponents. (Socialist realism, which has been the most
pronounced twentieth-century effort in this direction, has tended
to be a theory without much practice to exemplify it.) I have no
interest here simply in setting up and blowing down a straw-man
opponent. I have been imagining, as antagonistic to my interpretation of Herondas, a sophisticated and subtle realist, perhaps one
from the days of Zola and the Goncourt brothers, perhaps one
from our own day, like the critic and philosopher György Lukács.
That kind of antagonist, who might not be *very* antagonistic,
would be quick to fall on the seventh mime as confirmation of his
own point. It is high time we paid him the honor of trying to
appreciate his argument more clearly.

The present mime is fuller of the real things of its day than any
of the pieces considered so far; though saying this reminds us how
relatively little "hard information" of this kind Herondas ever
offers us. He is spare with details, and concentrates on the personalities in the foreground. We get here a list of shoes which,
though it sounds a little like the parody of an Homeric or Hesiodic
catalogue, nevertheless tells us a lot, once we can define its
words. And on the whole we can. We get considerable information about the price of commodities. One pair of shoes costs three
minae, another one mina, another seven. We get at least a general
feeling for the interior of a cobbler's shop, thus probably of many
small-business shops. On a slightly less concrete level we learn
something about the cobbler's profession; something which we
can add to what we learned in the sixth mime in order to arrive at
a larger opinion, which is not entirely complimentary. We learn
about shopping and bargaining customs. We learn a good deal to
add to our already growing knowledge of master-slave relations.
The realities we can find in this mime range from the concrete
(kinds of shoes) to social or economic interrelationships. There is

more of this kind of "information" in the seventh mime than in
most of the earlier ones, though we have by this time gained similar knowledge about a number of Alexandrian scenarios, living
rooms, temple precincts, law courts, private houses; as well as
about the kind of people inhabiting those places, and the practices
and assumptions of those people. To view Herondas as a "realist,"
in even a sophisticated sense of that term, must mean to think of
central importance, both to what Herondas intended and to what
he achieved, that he portrayed these realities of his society.

I have already tried to sketch, in this book, an alternate and I
think far more literarily relevant way of thinking about the way in
which an author internalizes his "experience" of his society; this
should help to make clear that Herondas was not simply portraying, or representing, his society. I don't at all mean to imply by
this point that the realities in mime seven are not real, or that the
knowledge we gain through reading about them is not real knowledge. It is not only "real" but it is important. I only want to suggest, again, that the knowledge in question is only a by-product of
the way in which Herondas makes his art.

IX *Mime Eight*

We come with this to the last complete (or nearly complete)
mime remaining to us from Herondas, and to that mime which
least comfortably fits into the picture of his other work.

The eighth mime is concerned primarily with a dream, the nature of which is so strange—thus helping us to enlarge our perception of Herondas—that I will quote the substance of it completely, and make some effort to analyze it in detail.

From the beginning, the *persona* of the poet is not identified
here. We are carried directly, and harshly, into his mind. He is
berating a slave. She is sleeping, not attending to duty. Then he
turns to a second slave, Megallis, and blames her bitterly for not
having the equipment for sacrifice ready in the house. Finally, he
turns to Annas, who seems to be more reliable, and asks him
please to "listen to my dream, for you don't keep such foolish wits
about you." Then he recounts the dream.

What he recounts, and the interpretation he gives of it, are
fairly familiar material in Alexandrian literary tradition. The
dream opens like this:

I fancied I was dragging a goat through a long dell, a goat of goodly beard and horns. And when need was, at break of day, for I was bested by weariness, I turned back and came forth from the glen at a spot where herdsmen at a sacrifice were filling the hollow with barley groats and fillets. And I robbed not, but the goat escaped me, and nibbled from one oak after another. But those around were right wrathful, and seized my goat, Annas, straightway as a spoil and tare it with their hands. And hard by me they came forward in conduct of their sports. There was a smooth-cheeked actor in slit frock of saffron, and part of the delicate rondure of his thigh was revealed to the beholder. He had girded on folds of fawn-skin mantles, with a linen shift reaching down from his shoulders, his head encircled with tendrils of ivy. Around his feet he had stretched golden high-boots with a lace. Such was his apparel: and one wore a wool-lining to guard against the chill of dawn, setting a waterproof cloak on his shoulders. (ll. 16–36)

To this point the dream is directly and "factually" described, not only without commentary, but as if no commentary could be necessary. We need to realize, though, that the references both to the goat and to the beautiful young actor would have indicated at once Dionysos and his rites. The country scene, with its dawn and chill, is the classic Dionysian setting. The action at the center of this dream soon begins:

A skin (you would call it that gift of Aeolus fatal to Odysseus's sailors,) did they set for a trail for all to leap thereon upright, and for a prize to the best, as we do in the revels to Dionysos. And some, plunging down on the dust, struck the earth amain with their foreheads, like divers; while others fell on their backs, and all, Annas, was mingled laughter and pain. And I thought that countless times, alone of all this wreck, I made the leap, and the spectators shouted applause as they saw the hide close evenly round me, and some declared me victor, but others. . . . (ll. 36–48)

At this point there are serious breaks in the manuscript. Reading it in its broken form we sense that we have reached a kind of climax here, in any case. The hectic action may refer to an actual skin-jumping rite, but it is so vivid and intense, in Herondas's account, that we can believe some actual dream-material is being turned up. In what follows there is a kind of break from the dream itself into rationalization. It goes on:

. . . A bowed dirty old man . . . to breathe out his fury, spurning
the sacred things of the gods? Out of my sight lest, old though I be, I
smite thee with the full force of my staff.

And I answered: —"Know, all ye who look on, I am ready to die for
the country, if the old man allows me. And I call the young man himself to witness." And he gave sentence that the officer should do away
with both. (ll. 50–64)

These lines bridge into the conclusion of the mime:

Here the vision ceased. Where is my coat? Give it here, Annas. This
is my dream and this its interpretation: —As I was dragging the goat
out of the dell and the herdsmen in their rites tare him amain and ate
the meat, right many henchmen of the muses shall rend asunder the
poems whereon I have a toiled—so I interpret. But whereas I fancied
that I alone won the prize, though many trod the air-tight skin, and in
that I made common cause with the old man in his wrath, great glory
shall I have from my verses, I swear by the Muses that adornest my
songs, that as a second venture dost make me to follow Hipponax of
old, and sign in crippled metre to the sons of Xouthos to be. (ll. 65–79)

Herondas—for we have little doubt that his *persona* represents
him directly here—is hurrying to press the point of his dream; and
in fact we hardly needed his explanation, except perhaps for
learning just a little more about his relation to the "old man." We
were quite aware that, in his dream, he was striding into the hard
arena of public controversy.

The generally accepted explanation of this entire mime is that it
shows Herondas plunged into the literary polemics of his day, and
in that sense that it reveals him as a person much more clearly
than any of his other extant pieces, in which he, as poet, always
appears carefully hidden behind his characters. This view is essentially correct.

At the end of the eighth mime the poet reveals his loyalty to
Hipponax, while earlier he had made it very clear that he considered himself superior, in competition, to his contemporary rivals.
Whether in fact our first impression is correct, that Herondas
turns up real subconscious material in his dream, it is certainly
true that he rationalizes the dream toward the end of the mime,

and infuses it with a purposefulness which is unmistakable. This is
the sense and way in which he brings himself to the front. That he
does so in this way invites us to go back over the major body of
his work in order to see what kind of presence he occupies in it.
How is Herondas in his work?

The question raised this way is subtle and difficult, yet it is
worth the trouble because providing an answer to it will be a big
step toward a restatement of the central theme of this chapter.

As we think back over the first mimes analyzed here we feel that
they have been sharply detached from the immediate presence of
their author. This is perhaps simply the detachment of drama; the
author disperses himself into a wide spectrum of scenes and characters, in all of which he is somehow present. However, these
mimes are very brief, and seem to be marked forcibly with their
author's character; so that it comes almost as a surprise to discover
that Herondas has in no place, during the first seven mimes, even
remotely referred to himself. His artifice is so considerable that
this abnegation fails to strike us at the time.

The eighth mime throws this earlier situation into obvious relief
and forces on us the consideration of just what kind of presence
Herondas is willing, at the most revealing, to assume in his work.
The eighth mime is a piece of literary controversy, I imagine, and
not a confession. Though it appears that perhaps there is some
actual dream-material being turned over here, still we do get the
sense of a literary temperament engaged with other writers, finding his confidence in himself, asserting his relationship to his literary ancestors; and, in general, striding onto the scene of his own
text as he had not done previously.

To understand these desires and personality-thrusts, in Herondas, is to understand better some of the motives with which he
must have put himself into creating his earlier mimes. He wanted
to establish scenes and he wanted to emulate his noble literary
predecessors. He wanted to shape a world for himself. Something
instinctive, and true to his medium, must have convinced him that
the most persuasive way to shape that world was to let it seem to
be shaping itself. That "letting it go," however, can only have
been permitted under conditions of the most intense supervision.
The supervision in question was the placement of the newly created literary-world into direct relation with a verbal and literary
tradition; thereby Herondas acquired for his new work a kind of

exemption from vulgar access, which at first sight, in any crudely "realistic" sense, might seem to be just the access the mimes invited.

X *Additions and Retrospect*

We have pitifully little more of Herondas than has been discussed to this point; he falls, like most ancient writers, into the fate of the mutilated. We have to reconstruct the scope of his thought and experience from the little that is preserved.

To be precise, there are a few more fragments in existence. Several of them will be mentioned in the following chapters, where they belong in brief discussions of the later writers who preserved these fragments, especially the anthologist Stobaios. Knox and Headlam optimistically entitle the longest of these remaining fragments *The Breakfast Party,* and do their best to conjecture what belonged in the enormous lacunae of the text.

Very little of this mime is preserved in a certain state. One lady is clearly addressing a group of ladies, and we can feel fairly certain she opens in this way:

Sit ye down, all. Where is baby? Give him here, Maie. Eueteira, give me Glyke too.

From what can be made of the remaining shreds of text, it looks as though the speaking lady assails and curses a servant girl and perhaps one of her own children. The problems of interpretation are almost insuperable, but Herondas has probably once again picked up his favorite preoccupations with gossiping women, disobedient brats, and even more disobedient servants. Where the rest of the tale went we are in no position to guess. Reading a fragmentary papyrus like this reminds us how narrowly Herondas as a whole escaped the oblivion of lacunae. A single papyrus is a narrow hold on life.

In the analyses of this chapter many kinds of interpretation, leading toward reconstruction, have been suggested, and it would be a mistake here to repeat any of those details. The overall argument has been clear, I hope, and was stated most explicitly at the beginning, where it was a question of establishing a definite perspective; I wanted there to emphasize the artificiality, artfulness, and historical consciousness of these mimes, and, by perhaps a slight exaggeration, to underplay the impression of stark realism which those mimes might at first seem to offer. (I say "slight" exaggeration for this reason, that if one comes on Herondas straight, say, from fifth century Greek literature, and if one is new to the Hellenistic period, one will inevitably get from Herondas an impression of intense immersion in everyday life.) In continuing the argument, though, I made some effort to fulfill and complete this earlier perspective, laying a good deal of stress on the contemporary character of the mimes. As in any literary criticism which in my way attempts to surround, and "account for," its object, I found myself having to proceed by an argument in stages, whereas the most appropriate address to the question would have been a simultaneous discussion of the multiple features of Herondas's work. In the following chapter, where I will try to look retrospectively onto Herondas's mimes, and briefly to locate them in the development of Western literature, it will be possible, at least in that new perspective, to give some thought to the global character of that ancient body of work, to the rounded shape in which it has presented itself to some of the minds which have in the last eighty or so years cared to interest themselves in Herondas.

CHAPTER 3

Literary Influences on the
Work of Herondas

> *History is not closed and does not reveal its origin.* Karl Jaspers, *The Unity of History*

I HAVE already said a little about the obscure topic reserved for this chapter. I will develop the matter here, both with regard to what was for Herondas his own literary heritage and with regard to some of his more influential contemporaries, like Theocritos. Whereas in the preface and first chapter I paid primary attention to cultural-historical questions, which established Herondas's own literary climate, I will now try to limit myself to literary matters. This will be appropriate, as we have just completed a fairly close look at the texts of Herondas's mimes.

We need to imagine that when Herondas turned back toward his own history in order to find inspiration, he was faced both with more and with fewer possibilities than face the writer today as he 'looks back.' Herondas had fewer possibilities only in the superficial, though important, sense that he had fewer books at his disposal; fewer private copies, fewer public places in which to consult texts. There were scroll libraries in every important city and Cos as a cultural center would have been no exception, while Alexandria was home to the world's largest concentration of books: but there were few large public libraries; the art of the scroll, which was cumbersome, bulky, and expensive, had advanced little since the Egyptian techniques of the fourth millennium B.C. Even when we balance, against all the disadvantages of the manuscript age, the astonishing energy and practice of the ancient memory, we still need to recognize the obstacles blocking the easy development of the ancient literary tradition.[1]

To counterbalance against this general problem, however, we need to reconsider another matter of the most decisive importance in the formation of ancient literary tradition, as of all European tradition to the time of the Renaissance. I mean the freedom with which, in those preprinting periods of our own cultural history, one author could directly draw on the words, phrases, techniques, stories, and inspirations of his own predecessors. There were no copyright laws to fear or even consider. (They begin to be passed and enforced in the sixteenth century, in England and on the European Continent; and are just recently, for interesting reasons, disappearing in some of the Communist countries.) But this is only the negative side of the question. There was in fact a climate, in the ancient cultural world, which strongly militated against a notion like that of copyright.[2]

Literary or artistic work in general was not looked on as the private property of its author. This was of course not entirely true. Literary work was far from anonymous. In fifth-century Athens there was an intense contest for the drama prizes which were awarded annually; and this competition itself, as well as the conditions for success in it, sprang from the distinctive personalities of the great dramatists who competed. The sculptors and architects of the time were doing the same, both figuratively and literally, by carving their names on their work. All of this suggests the literal truth of what of course we suspect; that ancient Greek art was importantly dominated by powerful personalities. Dominating even these personalities, however, was the notion that artistic material was public, not private, property, was what Horace later called *publica materies;* that the great devices, themes, and inspirations of Greek literature were in the public domain, to be used by anybody who was man enough to make use of them; that, to put it roughly, what was good in any art was absolutely good and should be used as well and as often as possible.[3] It is easy to see that this view could well be harmonized with that which puts strong individual personality at the center of artistic creation, for the *publica materies* view simply describes a context within which individual genius has to work. However the emphasis, within the notion of artistic public material, is very much on the desirability of artistic sharing and on willing reuse of the current artistic tradition.

This notion was alive in the Hellenistic period, and we can imagine Herondas standing fully inside it, as he cast his attention back onto his own literary heritage. It is true that by Hellenistic times there was more sense of the integrity of the book itself, and less reliance on the oral tradition, than there was in the fifth century, when book production was rarer and more expensive. But this was only a relative difference, insignificant when we contrast the general situation to any familiar from, say, post-Western Renaissance culture. It is no surprise to find Herondas drawing both generally and specifically, in direct phrasing, from the literature that offered itself to him as his past.

I Sophron, Hipponax, and Herondas

It may seem too general to mention Attic tragedy as the foundation of that literature which influenced him, but it is proper. Already in Homeric epic a pre-dramatic situation existed. Some two thirds of the *Iliad* and *Odyssey* are cast as speeches through and in which the characters address one another like characters in a drama. All the defining traits of the epic anchor this situation in narrative rather than drama, but the seeds of drama are planted there. It remains one of the moving and finally inexplicable data of world literature that in ancient Greece the epic transformed itself through the lyric, to make possible the birth of a new genus, drama, in which the seeds planted in epic could come fully to bloom. Although there was already, before the fifth century, a long rural ritual tradition in Greece, this did not come to complete development in literary terms until the time of Aeschylos. With him and his contemporaries came to birth the possibility of a primarily artistic (and primarily religious) presentation of figures in action on a stage. Whether or not Herondas's mimes were performed on a stage, they were indebted to the genuinely dramatic achievement of Greek tragedy for their very possibility of existence.

When we come to early Greek dramatic comedy we can be far more specific. The mimes of Sophron (ca. 460–420 B.C.) are probably, along with the satiric *choliambs* of Hipponax (mid-sixth century B.C.), the chief source of Herondas's work. We need to give some attention to the kinds of influence those two authors had on Herondas. To do this we have to fumble a little through the ruins of almost obliterated texts.

Sophron comes first here, not in time, but in order of probable importance to Herondas, for in his mimes Sophron seems to have opened the way for the small dialogue, the set dramatic piece to

be performed either as closet drama or as entertainment. It is no
wonder Plato slept with a copy of Sophron under his pillow.

What is left of Sophron tells us little. He is preserved only in
fragments—never more than two lines consecutively—embedded
in the work of other authors. From these pieces we can reconstruct almost nothing. The dialect is heavily Doric: Sophron was
from Sicily. The language springs from the guts:

1. he has the most odious hucksters near him,
1. into a huge cup he belches a triktus of anti-poison antidotes. . . .
3. a dog howling in front of the living room.[4]

And so on. Quoting at greater length, from the fragments collected by Kaibel (1899), would only mean multiplying examples
like these, and would bring us no closer to the relationship with
Herondas. In fact, it is hard to get much closer than this.
Sophron's language itself is prose, that is, without any apparent
metrical regularity of pattern. Yet as prose it is peppered with
colloquialisms, dialect, and talk taken from the mouths of ordinary urban citizens. It is this last trait, perhaps, that would most
have made Sophron seminal for the tradition which Herondas
adapted. The accomplishment involved here, in dipping far into
popular speech for literary purposes, is likely to be hard for us to
appreciate. Many centuries of modern and colloquialized literary
tradition have gone into creating our attitude. But the accomplishment must have been fairly difficult, even as late in Greek
literary history as the time of Sophron. When we remember that
he wrote "prose," it will seem that he made, in his mimes, a meaningful break with the purely literary style in Greek literature.

We need to add, to the other aspects of this break, a final important point which however we can hardly back up from the
extant text of Sophron, but only from the available secondary evidence. Choricius, in his apology for the mime, for its vulgarity,
which evidently linked it, in Sicily, to pretty coarse country ritu-
als, lists the following stock characters of the early mime, of
Sophron's time: "a man lecturing his wife, soldiers, two orators—
one unreasonable and one sensible, masters, slaves, petty trades-
men, sausage-sellers, cooks, *hestiatores* (hosts), *daitymones*
(guests), *symbolaia graphontes* (contract writers), a lisping
child, a young man in love, one angry and another placating his

anger." [5] Whether Sophron offered quite this wide bill of fare we can no longer know, but in any case that is not the main question. What matters is to see the theory of literary type-characters appearing here. We know already how important the heritage of this theory was for Herondas's work.

Hipponax is an almost equally shattered source of our knowledge about Herondas's tradition. Fortunately, though, we still have what seem to be several complete examples of his work, so that we can at least begin to hear his tone. And in almost all the individual separate fragments, unintelligible as they may be in most respects, we can at least catch the sound of those choliambs, limping iambs, which Hipponax was the first to prepare for literary use, and Herondas one of the last to use successfully.

Hipponax was famous as a parodist and ridiculer, and that gift of his, joined to his prosody, recommended him to Herondas. A look at one of his poems will suggest this quality in the earlier, sixth-century poet.We can start with a transliteration, to show the prosody.

> Dŭ hémĕraí gŭnaíkŏs eísĭn hédĭstaĭ,
> hŏtán gămé tĭs kákphĕré tĕthnékuĭăn.

Each line is regular iambic until its last foot, at which point it counteracts its own motion, becoming trochaic. We know this line well from Herondas, in whom its effect is equally, but differently, startling; in whom it slows down narrative, calling it back to the raw material of the individual line. It is of the greatest interest to see this prosodic device working in two such different poets, at such different times. The "semantic meaning" of the present distich is something like this:

> There are two happiest days for a woman,
> when she marries and when they carry her out dead.

We don't know whether this is a parody. (Locating parody is hard enough even in one's own time; it is almost impossible in the case of Greek literature, except when the most famous texts are being rehandled.) But the note of satire is certainly here, wrapped up somewhere in the social criticism; perhaps nourished by that criticism, as happened in the poetry of Juvenal and Samuel Johnson and in the painting of Hogarth and Toulouse-Lautrec. It is a note for which some considerable preparation was required in Greek literature, and for which at the time of Hipponax we have no extant precedent in that literature except the *Margites*, a comic epic, and the *Battle of the Frogs and Mice*. This satire literature, and the parodies it includes, seems generally to have had its roots in native country soil, and to have behind it a considerable tradition of rather vulgar popular dramatic acts. It is interesting to see how healthily those traditions survived into Alexandrian times. Herondas and Theocritos probably drew, for their senses of the popular, vulgar, or rustic, far more on ancient literary traditions than on contemporary folk traditions. (Literature is to a surprising extent, as we are always rediscovering, as much about literature as about life: Bacchylides was so to a great extent about Pindar, Terence about Menander, Dryden about Ben Jonson, and so on.)

When we get past Hipponax, Sophron, and tragedy, in search of literary influences on Herondas we come headlong against two kinds of classic problem. The one is relatively uninteresting, though very important: it is simply that we have very little ancient Greek literature left, that we can find few influences at all within the body of that literature. The more interesting problem is that raised whenever we discuss literary influence. There is a large, inexpensive, and fairly harmless sense of this term in which we can readily see many influences of any particular Greek author. In that sense I spoke of Attic tragedy as a kind of influence. It would have been going much too far, however, to include Homer as an influence even in this wide sense. When we come to Sophron and Hipponax as influences we are in difficult waters. It is partly ancient testimony which leads us to these conclusions about ancient literary influence; and usually, as in the present case, we find the testimony based on solid tradition and accurate judgment. But if ancient tradition is surprisingly accurate in that sense, it is almost always uncritical in another sense; though it is hardly more uncritical than modern historians of literature have tended often to be. How uncritical it is we can see simply by reflecting on the few examples involved here: Sophron, Hipponax, and Herondas.

These figures are divided from one another by wide gaps in time, by the vast differences in the literary kinds which they were writing, and by the differences in the kinds of audience they envisaged; none of these problems are brought up by the ancient critics. Their negligence is understandable, especially since questions of this kind were both difficult and hard to investigate considering the evidence—almost wholly biographical, not at all 'sociological'—which was available to the ancient critic. But it is less easy to see how they, the writers of testimonia and biographical criticism, failed to see the inapplicability of their kind of criticism to the literary issues themselves.

II *The Question of Influence Itself*

When Hipponax and Sophron have been aligned, and called "influences on Herondas," of what value is this point to us for a deeper or more extensive understanding of Herondas? What can we learn from the examples collected already in this chapter, and which were precisely the kinds of example collected by the ancient critics?

We learn to see similarities. The earthiness and proverbial spirit of Sophron; the prosody and satirical punch of Hipponax: we learn to use these tags to describe the common properties of the writers. We can accept the fact that Herondas drew some of his disposition and verbal strategy from these earlier writers. What does this help us to see in Herondas? I think there is an answer, which may at first seem banal but which soon, in fact, turns out to introduce a remarkable paradox.

The answer is simply that the kinds of argument, which the ancient critics (and I and others) are proposing, are ways of drawing our attention to the main features of Herondas, to those 'common properties' I just mentioned. This kind of drawing of attention is important and valuable; and within a given field of explanation—a given national literature, a given botanical genus—members who are close to and precede other members are likely to be of peculiar value for 'explaining,' or 'giving an account of' the item one wants to attend to. The paradox I mention is this: that the items—in this case the works of literature—which *follow* one's particular concern, Herondas, are likely to be as relevant to 'explaining' the main concern, as the works which precede it. This paradox may be one only because it counters our too habitual idea of explanation by historical causality, by genesis in time. To my knowledge, Christian theology has done a great deal to set our models for a counter theory; as, for instance, in showing how the significance of Jesus Christ is chiefly intelligible in terms of what effect he had on our world. The field of explanation is greatly widened by this perspective. We can return to some of its implications in the next chapter when we consider the sense in which the 'meaning' of Herondas's work is only completed by the effects it had later on scholars, poets, and anyone else who accepted the weight of that earlier achievement in language. (We speak only of Herondas, though any example from literary history would be equally appropriate.)

The purpose of this digression is not to undercut the orthodox method of studying literary influence, a method which was implicitly at work in my earlier comments about Hipponax and Sophron, and which must continue to underlie a great deal of literary scholarship in its effort to promote understanding. The reason for digressing was in part to make the method at work here conscious of itself and to expose not only its limits but its own philosophical assumptions; and in part—as in the last comments of the preceding paragraph—to suggest some of the alternative revisions to which the orthodox perspective can easily afford to submit itself.

III   Detailed Examples of Influence on Herondas

Many further examples of earlier influence on Herondas all bring us back more or less directly into the question of method. I have chosen three very detailed examples, which raise only slightly different aspects of the question of influence; it should in this way be possible for us to get farther into both the practical and theoretical implications of this problem.

The first example is rare; it gives us a much more direct and concrete reference-back than we usually find in Herondas's lines. The evidence is easy to assemble. In Mime Three (ll. 66–67) Herondas has the Schoolmaster threaten Kottalos with the following:

I'll make you more orderly than a girl, stirring not a twig, if that's what you're after.

Just the same combination of phrases occurs in Aristophanes (*Lysistrata*, l. 473); the rough translation of the Chorus' speech there is:

Since I want to sit in an orderly way like a girl, feeling no pain, moving not a twig. . . .

There are two nearly direct verbal parallels here: "Moving not a twig" (*kinounta* or *kinousa mede karphos;* and the phrase about "making one, or sitting, more orderly than [or like] a girl." (In the second phrase a single idiom, "more orderly than a girl" is embedded in two different versions.) In the two passages as wholes, however, the use made of these verbal raw materials is entirely different. In the passage from Herondas the schoolmaster is threatening Kottalos. In Aristophanes the chorus of women is telling the chorus of old men about the revenge they, the men, can expect when they try to make love to the ladies.

Is Herondas revealing the influence of Aristophanes here? It is extremely difficult to know, when we come down from literary-historical generalities to details like this. It is entirely possible that there is a direct, slightly witty, carefully planned verbal reuse here, which would have been intelligible to an educated Alexandrian audience. If Herondas's mimes were recited aloud, which is possible and I think likely, they would certainly have been heard by audiences accustomed to attending theatrical performances of Aristophanes and the Greek tragedians; and there is no reason to doubt that, in a still fairly bookless culture, the audience's ears would have been at least passively attuned to lines like these from Aristophanes. In that case they would certainly have felt the resistance against those lines, and the counterplay with them, which Herondas manipulates.

We can also speculate in the other direction. The phrases in question may—and we can't really know—have been the most ordinary commonplaces of spoken Greek. They may not have stood out in any relief at all here. Herondas may have known little of Aristophanes.

In raising these questions we are taking a position even farther removed from the actual text of Herondas than we do when we consider what we learn, from proven influences on him, for the understanding of his text. We are now simply discussing possible influence. In such cases, and Herondas like many other later Greek authors offers many, it is idle to guess whether the influence is actual. When scholarship becomes a guessing game we should leave it alone. It is here only worth assuming the reality of the relationship, then using it to establish a new field of meanings, in terms of which to understand the texts involved. This *as if* process need not involve self-deception; it may in fact bask in the awareness of the speculative risk it is taking, and the inherent possibilities for new penetration of texts. What matters in such operations is, after all, understanding of works of art.

The second detailed, this time very detailed, example raises again the question not only of the significance of influence but also the question whether influence has taken place. (The difficulty of expressing that image is a key to our embarrassment when it comes to a close discussion of influence.) In Mime Six, where the ladies chat cozily about a *baubon*, Koritto is praising Kerdon's workmanship. She says:

> . . . he brought two of them with him, Metro—at first glance my eyes swelled out of my head; I may tell you,—we are alone—, they were firmer than the real article, and not only that, but as soft as sleep. . . . (ll. 67–71)

The strange beauty of the last image, "soft as sleep," strikes us even when we come on the line in English. At once it reminds us how little poetic language we are used to finding in Herondas; how few images, for instance. While it is possible that Herondas might have coined the present expression, it is more likely that he picked it up out of his literary heritage, or, a little less likely, from the air of popular speech. Headlam and Knox say (p. 307) that "the simile was made possible by the Homeric epithet *malakos* of sleep." The first passage they refer to, by way of explanation, is the second line of *Iliad X:*

> The other best men of the Acheans slept all night by their ships, bound by soft sleep. (My translation.)

They go on citing the first usage in which this simile is converted into a simile embodying a comparative degree of the adjective for soft, softer: for instance, Eustathios (785.55) speaks of

> the speaker taking from them blankets softer than sleep . . . or Theocritos (XV, 125) speaks of "purple blankets softer than sleep."

Again we face the double-headed question: has there been influence, and of what interest is it? That there has been influence we can certainly not prove here, and it would be futile in any case to attach it to a single source. On the other hand we seem to have a literary image here, one treated and polished by literary tradition, and in that way meaningful to Herondas's hearers. That Homer made this simile possible is probably attributing more importance to literature, in forming a language, than is reasonable, even in the case of Homer's domination over Greek literature. But it is one way of saying how important literature is in establishing the possibilities of a language. In that sense all the language users who prepared this image for Herondas were preparing it to influence him. In the present case we can also see the interesting end-result of such chains of verbal inheritance. Herondas embeds the image in a totally different context from that of his other literary predecessors. Certainly there is some irony, if there is any literary influence here at all, in the use to which he puts the idyllic beauty of this image.

The third example I choose is literarily richer, though it still involves only a very few lines. This time the historical reference back into influencing literature is unquestionable, though the range of possible reference is wide, and nothing leads us to make it more precise. At the end of his defense, the Pander (Mime Two) reminds the jurors of Cos that in voting for him

you will prove the might of Cos and Merops; and the glory of Thessalos and Herakles, and the cause of Asklepios's coming hither from Tricca and the reason wherefore Rhode bare Leto on this spot. (ll. 95–98)

The hearer or reader of these lines took them as a parody of those patriotic perorations which were common enough at the end of legal speeches in Greece. A close reader would have noticed, furthermore, how carefully the present references are worked out; how carefully Herondas was constructing his parody, and indirectly his own panegyric, the kind he put in the mouth of the old woman who praised Egypt in the first mime. The references are exact, minute, and learned; as in the reference to Thessalos, who was the child of Khalkiope by Herakles, when Herakles stopped

at Cos on the way back from the Trojan War; or in the reference
to the very obscure report about Leto's birth on Cos, a rumor
supported, in the literature we know, only by a passage in Tacitus,
which is obviously echoing some earlier tradition familiar to
Herondas.

Close attention to this passage would have reminded the contemporary reader, confusedly, of a number of speeches on whose
strategy Herondas probably was drawing for this crafty parody,
which included his own private peroration. Verbal strategies of
this kind were commonplace in Attic oratory. One of the most
common sources of such rhetoric was the patriotic funeral oration,
whose origins reach back to the earliest period of Greek culture,
and whose highest achievements, as in Pericles's oration reported
by Thucydides, became cultural rallying points for a whole
people. The flourishing of oratory within the century before Herondas's life had made common those sentiments of highly articu-
late patriotism which seem, no matter how eloquently they are
refurbished, inevitably to lose their life, and to invite irony. Herondas's hearers or readers could not have forgotten such patriotic
funeral orations as Lysias's to the Athenian soldiers who fell fight-
ing against Corinth between 394 and 386; or Demosthenes's *On
the Crown* (330), in which he supports his attack against the dishonest Aeschines by drawing attention to the famous integrity of
Athens, an integrity proven by the fearless conduct of Athenian
soldiers who had through the years unquestioningly died for their
polis. We may seem, here, to be reaching back toward chauvinistic
examples drawn from a sphere of language and intention far removed from that invoked by Battaros before the jury at Cos. But
Herondas is certainly playing with both similarity and difference
here. He is genuinely parodying the tradition on which he is
drawing for his literary effect.

IV *Herondas and Theocritos*

The question of influence has presented itself here in several
forms. Sophron and Hipponax were taken to be whole literary
achievements, embodiments of personality in form, which offered
something to Herondas's sense of his craft and its possibilities.
After touching on those relatively large, but terribly obscure,
sources of influence we went to the opposite extreme: to three
detailed instances of influence. We looked into a couple of idioms

from Aristophanes, a simile with roots in Homer, and a trope of chauvinistic praise familiar to the Attic orators. In none of these detailed examples—and I think this would have been true wherever we looked into the question—was there anything like a clearcut case of influence in the most orthodox sense. (That sense which may actually be more a myth than we realize; for when we look for theorists, who believe in any kind of dominance of source over literary receiver, we find almost no one. The French Professors of the *Revue de Littérature Comparée* in the 1920's—men like Fernand Baldensperger and Paul Van Tieghem—come as close as any to defending this position; but their exercise of it is supple and literary, rarely authoritarian.) We were simply setting up models for the literary strategies which Herondas employed, and in doing so we were treating Herondas's sources in the way we would treat Herondas himself if we took him as a source. Then we were inviting those models to help us look closely at what Herondas was doing. Influence was the realm of freshly acquired intelligibility which we won by seeing into these interrelationships.

When we arrive nearer to Herondas's own time, we find him entering into literary relationships, with immediate predecessors or with contemporaries, of which it is in many cases impossible to say whether influence has in any sense taken place. The complexity and interest of this problem can probably be brought out best by comparing Theocritos's *Idyll XV* with Herondas's fourth mime. We will look at that comparison in a moment.

First, though, we need to review a question touched earlier, about the relation of Herondas to Menander and Theophrastos. What was said there about stock characters, and about a new concern for the typical in literature, applies here. A great deal happened, even to the possibilities for the mime, between the accomplishments of Sophron and Hipponax and those of Herondas. Of most importance, perhaps, was the new double awareness: of the particularity of the stock character, the eccentric character, fused with a new sense of the generality, and often symbolic or even allegorical, meaning of that character.

In Theophrastos we see a "psychological" grounding for the sense of a social world which divides itself up into such characters as Menander or Herondas, or even Theocritos, put in motion in their poetic works. In Menander we see a working out of these

implications rather as they are worked out in Shakespeare's comedies. This is the case, for instance, in Menander's *Dyscolos,* that
play which was first discovered in 1957, in the sands of Egypt.
(Who knows what else those sands will give us if they are allowed
to surface their matter in peace?) The play is dominated by a
bitter old curmudgeon who learns wisdom and humanity through
the discovery of his dependence on other people. He is surrounded by a faithful, attractive daughter and a classic protective
shrew of a house servant. He (and his daughter) are assailed by a
neighbor's servant (the stock figure Davus), a smooth, comic
suitor of his daughter, and an end-man ally of the suitor. I don't
want to press my analogy of this situation with situations occurring frequently in Herondas. But the social world taken for
granted here is obviously close to that found in Herondas.

With Theocritos, probably an exact contemporary of Herondas,
the parallels are much closer; though both he and Herondas draw
something, for their view of literature and its characters, from the
generalizing assumptions of Menander, as well certainly as from
his closeness to the ordinary details of daily middle-class life.
Idylls II, XIV, and XV of Theocritos, are commonly supposed to
have their sources in Sophron, though this is only ancient rumor.
When we read these pieces we are startled by their many similarities to Herondas. We don't know certainly which poet influenced
the other, or whether both drew on the same source, probably
Sophron; but there is an indication, based on evidence too detailed to fit here, that Herondas was heavily in debt to Theocritos.

We need to look toward Theocritos briefly. Whatever our judgment on the evidence of influence, we will agree that this relationship was one which draws our attention to both the writers involved.

The three idylls in question—and many more of Theocritos's
poems—all either in monologue or dialogue present scenes from
daily life. The second idyll is the passionate, sensuous plea of
Simaitha for the return of her lover, who has recently forgotten
her, and whom—though she still loves him—she will poison to
death if he can't bring himself to return. The fourteenth idyll is a
dialogue in which Aeschines explains to Thyonichos what makes
him so sad, that his girl friend Kyniska has abandoned him, and
has made this painfully clear at a rustic festival, in which she refused to toast Aeschines. At the end Thyonichos advises his friend

to go off to the splendid city of Ptolemy in Egypt, to the king who is "of good heart, a lover of the Muses, a *galant,* sweet-tempered to the highest degree. . . ." The fifteenth idyll is the most complex of the three. *The Syracusan Women* consists of three scenes: in the first Gorgo and Praxinoa are getting dressed to go out to a street festival; in the second scene they are talking to each other while they are being jostled in the streets; in the final scene they are looking at tapestries and listening to a song in Ptolemy's royal residence.

If we restrict ourselves simply to these three pieces we see much in common with Herondas. The thematic and characterizing parallels are startling. We know the jealous lover—in Herondas's fifth mime Bitinna is done to perfection—in both poets. Each poet grasps the despair of love strongly, though they do this very differently from one another. Theocritos's Simaitha is far more delicate, despairing, and less depraved than Bitinna. Where Herondas tells us this in choliambs, Theocritos does so in straight iambs. Where Herondas gives us a playlet, which was probably performed, Theocritos gives us a monologue, probably not performed. Yet the Hellenistic mime and the Hellenistic idyll are very close to one another. When the themes are as close as in the two pieces in question, we are certain to learn more about each of them by juxtaposing them. By doing so we will inevitably be able to feel, more than we can quite analyze, the similar moods of compassionate but slightly detached social portrayal which these two poets establish.

The fourteenth idyll ends on a praise of Ptolemy which is startlingly close to that offered by the old nurse in Herondas's first mime. Herondas may well have learned something from Theocritos about how to integrate such material into a tale, something which Theocritos characteristically, and in the present case as well, is defter at than Herondas. Again lost love unites Theocritos's fourteenth idyll with the theme of more than one mime, though here the comparison helps us to notice a strikingly different trait of Herondas. When it comes to romance or eros, Herondas seems almost exclusively interested in the problems of women.

The most thoroughgoing and instructive parallel is between Theocritos's fifteenth idyll and the fourth mime of Herondas, in which Kynno and Kokkale are sacrificing in the temple of Asklepios. The tone of the two women, Kynno and Kokkale, is precisely

that of Gorgo and Praxinoa as they are jostled in the festive
crowd of a procession for Adonis: in both pieces the tone of vulgar, vital, current speech is picked up; a Damon Runyan tone, an
O. Henry tone. It is almost painfully accurate, and much closer to
the bone of real life, I think, than anything in earlier Greek literature. (By contrast, Menander seems rhetorical; and the fifth-
century dramatists seem distant and ritual, even if much greater
than their fourth-century successors.) Even the relationships between the two women are similar; one woman more forceful and
acute, the other more awe-struck and full of questions. The second section of Theocritos's idyll gives the sense of a turbid Greek
crowd; and in the third, in which the women are looking at a
gorgeous fresco, we feel involved in their world. Once again our
attention is simply drawn, by the startling resemblance to Herondas, to the virtual uniqueness of these two authors, ancient Greek
realists.

Even before discussing Theocritos we had considered many
possible relationships under the heading of influence on Herondas. We have now with Theocritos reached a point at which—
though even that is not certain—every orthodox meaning of influence on Herondas seems to be excluded. Theocritos appears,
where he relates at all to Herondas, to coincide with him strongly,
to seem not to have exerted influence but to have worked parallel
to his contemporary. Even this relationship, however, is potentially of the greatest value in helping us to understand what Herondas is doing. The core of that point has already been exposed; that
we see Herondas, like Theocritos, working out from a certain
mood, perception, and atmosphere which is part of his own time.
When we consider the difficulty simply of *locating* ancient Greek
works, of making them reveal their local, specific character, we
see the special value of understanding the interrelation between
Herondas and Theocritos.

CHAPTER 4

The Influence of Herondas

> . . . they are (at least partially) right
> who situate the crown of evolution in
> a supreme act of collective vision ob-
> tained by a panhuman effort of inves-
> tigation and construction. Teilhard de
> Chardin, *The Phenomenon of Man*

WE come now to a topic which is either microscopic or vast, according to our perspective. If we are looking for the literary influence of Herondas we will find almost nothing; partly, at least, because of the lateness of the rediscovery of Herondas's text. No classical author who was dormant during the Renaissance stands much chance of exercising influence on creators; for the Renaissance set the modern canons of status and influence, and drew attention to its classical favorites. Herondas played no part in that.

However, there has been a great deal written *about* Herondas, since the time of his new birth in 1890. Most of this literature about him has been scholarship; there has in fact been little written about Herondas that wasn't a serious effort to understand his text or his times, that wasn't what we consider "serious scholarship." Is there any reason not to consider that scholarship part of the influence of Herondas, part of the influence he has exerted?

I hope it has been clear, from the beginning of this book, that I consider scholarship part of the record of such influence. Emphasizing the point in that way would be unnecessary except for our prejudices about the split between the scholarly and the creative as modes of keeping an author alive, of supporting him through re-experience.

A moment's reflection on the word *about*, as applied to scholarship "on" an ancient author, may introduce the matter freshly here. Such *writing about* can mean many things, while it nevertheless remains part of what we normally call scholarship: it can designate activities ranging from external and quantitative accounts of what is in an author's work, where he was born, and so on, to activities like writing into the essential spirit of that author, or raising critical questions of value about his work. To confine the term scholarship to either of those activities would be unnecessarily rigid. It would be equally rigid to draw a sharp line between the second kind of scholarship and the work a creative writer might do in taking up the spirit of Herondas, or any author, into himself. (And we know that such a "taking up" is the most common strategy of the writer.) I am speaking abstractly now, and will try to prove my point in this chapter. I think it will become clear that the living tradition of Herondas scholarship—a small and elite thrust even within the small field of Hellenic scholarship—has been nourished by a very substantial negotiation with both the spirit and the stuff of Herondas's poetry.

When we reach our own times, which we will almost immediately do, I will try to look into a number of examples of Herondas scholarship which are about Herondas in a creative sense. In doing this I will be sharply selective, choosing to consider a few from the already large number of works, mostly articles, on Herondas. I will try to meet my own thesis at its most difficult point, by devoting considerable attention to the four editions of Herondas, in four major languages, which have been mentioned earlier. We will be able to see, there, some of the workings of the poetry of textual criticism, that criticism which in every word choice, in every chosen reading, commits itself to a view of the meaning and structure of a particular work. Pedantry is pedantry, even in a poem; but scholarship is a human art, at least far more so than our clichés about it normally allow us to realize.

I *Ancient Testimonies to Herondas*

We soon exhaust the ancient testimonies to Herondas, though there are a number of incidental references to him which are hardly worth discussion here. What we must mention is little. The most substantial testimony is from Pliny the Younger. It comes almost as a relief to have the existence and importance of Herondas confirmed by such a reliable authority. The comment is from around 100 A.D.

To his friend Arrius Antonius, who as consul has been stationed in what the Romans called Asia, in close proximity to Greek culture, Pliny writes:

I had this impression (of great skill and felicity) when I read your Greek epigrams; when I recently read your mimiambs. How much humanity and charm they contain, how sweet and lovable and sharp and accurate they are! I would have thought I was reading Callimachus or Herondas, or something better than these—if there is anything.[1]

The remark is so offhand that it suggests how well-known Herondas must have been in Roman literary circles, three hundred and fifty years after his death, roughly the length of time that has elapsed between Herrick or Marvell and us. This measure gives us a rough sense of the amount of fame required to last that long.

The other available allusions back into Herondas, from Latin literature, are so little developed, and so rare, that they are a source of a special kind of surprise, a surprise that in fact an author so distinguished in Pliny's opinion should have aroused so little comment in Rome. Only one explanation for this surprise comes to mind: the mime (as in Herondas) was a form little used in Rome, and known to the Romans chiefly in the very difficult form of Herondas's Greek. There may simply have been few Roman men of letters who could read, understand, and re-experience Herondas. Two of those men deserve mention here: Virgilius Romanus and Gaius Matius.

The case of Gaius Matius and Herondas is illustratively obscure, and I have left it until after Pliny simply for that reason; although Matius seems to have lived and written about the beginning of the first century B.C. We know that he wrote mimiambs, iambic verse fit for mimes, and that is already a strong reason to suppose he knew Herondas's work. (He also wrote a literal translation of the *Iliad* and a cookbook, which became so famous that the Romans named a hash after him.) Already in the Renaissance Scaliger guessed that the choliambs of Matius were based on a literal translation of Herondas. That they were a translation at all, however, is far from certain. If they were, they translated a collection of Herondas's mimes which began with number eight, and perhaps included as many more mimes as we now have, among

them, possibly, those from which we still have fragments enough
to form a slight impression, those called "The Breakfast Party,"
"Factory Girls," and "Molpinos" (cited by Stobaios).[2] The issues
involved, in deciding whether Matius translated, or even knew,
Herondas are delicate and detailed; and not worth attention except as illustrations of the kind of problem often raised by the
study of influence in ancient literature; a subject some of whose
complexities I touched on in the previous chapter. It is a question,
for instance, of examining Latin choliambs like

> iam iam albicascit Phoebus, et recentatur
> commune lumen hominibus voluptatis

> (now Phoebus brings dawn again, and the common
> light of pleasure returns to men)

or

> sinuque amicam refice frigidam caldo
> columbulatim labra conserens labris

> (with your hot breast warm your girl
> pressing your lips like a dove to her);[3]

and trying to set them up against isolated lines of Herondas. In
this case, admitting it as pure conjecture, Knox suggests putting
the earlier line, with its sententious wisdom, together with the
"Molpinos," of which four lines remain; while the second line
might go with "The Factory Girls," might fit with what is perhaps
a conversation among prostitutes. True, they are rather literary
lines for prostitutes. It should be obvious, by the way, that there is
great room for finesse, or lack of it, in this kind of scholarship. The
present tiny example illustrates the sense in which good scholarship cannot afford to cut itself off from the felt interior of the
works it is considering.

Of Virgilius Romanus we have nothing left but a reference in
Pliny the Younger who says that

> he wrote mimiambs delicately and most beautifully,
> and in this genre he wrote most eloquently. . . .[4]

He also wrote, the passage goes on to say, comedies in the manner of Menander, comedies worthy to be "counted among those of Plautus and Terence." Admittedly, this gives us little to go on. However, we know of Pliny's admiration for Herondas the mimiambist; and we can feel certain that the present reference to Virgilius includes an echo of remembrance of Herondas.

Beyond that point we are confined to quotations from Herondas. In a vast *Anthology* of beloved passages, collected around 500 A.D. from many ancient Greek authors, Stobaios gives us four lines of what we may look on as the tenth mime of Herondas. Those lines are:

> Gryllus, Gryllus, then you have passed your sixtieth
> sun, die and become ashes; since thenceforward the
> last lap of life is blind; for already the light of
> being is dimmed.[5]

The thought is probably from the beginning of the mime called 'Molpinos,' mentioned above, and is certainly an echo of a thought fairly common in Greek poetry; Mimnermos had been followed by many in his advice that men should not live past sixty. As far as our understanding of Herondas goes, we should only add that the tone of address to Gryllos differs from the usual tone even of Herondas's dialogue; here it is more emphatic and more didactic. It is likely, I suppose, that if in fact there were originally some double the number of mimes we now possess, there must have been more variety of tone than is now suggested by what remains of Herondas. We began to sense this clearly, already in the Dream-Mime; but the present fragment confirms the suspicion.

In another fragment Stobaios leaves us these four tantalizing and unlocated lines, which he attributes to "the mimiambs of Herondas":

> Now he plays "blind cow," now "hit the pot,"
> now he lets beetles fly on strings
> from my tow [?] and completely mixes
> up the head of my spinning-wheel.[6]

Crusius is reminded of the third mime by these lines. It is hard to say more than that about them.

II *Herondas and Modern Textual Scholarship*

From this point we leap across centuries. The next significant references to Herondas are heard after the rediscovery of manuscripts in Egypt in 1890. We are now in the world of modern scholarship, a system of analytical-rational-intuitive assumptions of a total character not formerly put together and developed in Western culture. We need to pause a moment, if only to catch breath. We are encountering a change, within scholarship, that both fosters and discourages its relationship to the creative, that at least in one sense makes possible the wider experience of the scholarly which crosses the orthodox boundaries between scholarship and creative work.

It is interesting to consider the themes which have dominated scholarship on Herondas from 1891 to our day. There is considerable work on the establishment of texts, quite naturally, at this stage in simply working up and presenting the material. Crusius, Herzog, Nairn, Headlam, Puccioni, and many others, are busy and have been busy with this. This is the period during which a consolidation begins which will continue all through the life of the original author's text. (The original Greek text is quite literally never a settled matter. Every new edition of Aeschylos or Euripides or Pindar is swollen with emendations.) But already at this stage there are various other kinds of work going on, an interesting indication that it is not necessary for a text to be settled before it can be criticized. There is some translation, the earliest published into English by Sharpley (1906), into Polish by Winkowski (1900), into French by Quilland (1900); and there have been others since. Finally, there is a good deal of philological, chiefly linguistic, grammar-based, commentary. The purpose of the translation is already explicitly literary; the philology is on the level of text-establishment and text-understanding, as it verges toward aesthetic reliving. We can look into these three categories of Herondas scholarship and will have no trouble realizing that these scholars, through their work, are taking a stand inside Herondas, genuinely bearing his influence farther.

The first concern of Herondas scholarship has always been textual and editorial. The same holds for scholarship on earlier Greek authors, but in modern times we seldom have the chance to see this textual process worked out before our eyes; it is usually already part of the history of scholarship on a particular author. I have referred to the awe we can feel, in the presence of the original manuscript of Herondas. Now I refer to the serious difficulties involved in transcribing it. Kenyon, in his preface to the first printing of the Herondas manuscript (1891), writes graphically about the original document:

For the most part, the papyrus is sound, and the writing clear and in good condition; but in many places, especially toward the end, it has been considerably eaten by worms, and in others the writing has been rubbed, which causes the text of some of the poems to be seriously mutilated.[7]

As we glance over the facsimile we see how understated even this last sentence remains. The hand is clear but the fabric is worn even as far as the center of the column, and in some places farther.

It will help, toward sharpening the force of this point, if we concentrate very pedantically on a few of the variant readings that arose in the years shortly after 1891 in efforts to establish a text of the first few lines of the first mime. I am thinking of the editions made by Rutherford (1891), Crusius (1894), and Nairn (1904). The edition by Kenyon (1891), referred to above, aims only to present a facsimile, with no conjectures, variant readings, or filled lacunae, but with a normalized, printed transcription; anyone but an epigrapher will have to check these three texts against Kenyon as base, and can feel confident he is getting the unglossed difficult version bequeathed him by an Egyptian scribe.

The initial problems are obvious enough. The first word of the first speech, Metriche's, is partly obliterated: we are left with theta (θ) followed by four blank spaces—the hand is orderly enough that we can usually judge how much has been lost—and then, by sigma alpha: and the problem is easily solvable because of a later reference to a Threissa who is clearly identical with the woman in the first line. Even here, interestingly enough, there is a slight variation in readings: Rutherford—but on what authority I don't know—dropped the last letter, the alpha, of Threissa's name; with the result, which of course he wanted for the sake of euphony, that the elision which naturally would have occurred here before the alpha at the beginning of the following word, that the phonetic elision would be represented by the orthography. It is hard to see any justification for this procedure. The final alpha of *Threissa* is clearly there on the papyrus. But the case, though small and detailed, is not unworthy of mention, for interpretation enters at every level in this kind of textual work. Rutherford himself is ready to adopt, as guide toward a good many of his changes, the justification that Herondas's "dialect has suffered sadly in transmission, being in some things almost consistently atticized, except that just enough evidence is left to show the atticizing up" (p. ix); an argument which though at many points hard to attack is an invitation to fantasy as well as to creative interpretation. No good edition can get by, however, without some larger grid of interpretation, like Rutherford's, within which to plan the specific problem of deciphering posed by the manuscript or papyrus. The editor's job, after all, is not only to copy correctly, which requires enough finesse, but to restore, when necessary to see the mistakes made by the copier and to rectify them.

Another kind of problem arises in the third line; a problem caused not only by unclear orthography and papryus, and the problems associated with that problem, but also by the papyrus's failure to indicate changes in speaker. Like all ancient poetry texts this one runs on, respecting only line endings, offering no punctuation, capitalizing, or identation; with a disregard, for what is in effect built-in running commentary, that seems to reflect a view of written language different from ours, perhaps a view of it closer to continuous, unbroken speech than we usually take written language to be. The third line is clearly opened by Threissa, who breaks in on these lines of Metriche:

> Threissa, someone is knocking, won't you see
>   whether someone has come to us from the country?

with (in literal order):

who [knocked on] the door:

followed by

> who are you? are you afraid
>   to come nearer? (spoken by Threissa to Gyllis).

The problem is once again raised by Rutherford, who has taken a variant position; and one which in this case is probably interestingly wrong. For the *I* attributed to Gyllis in line three, Rutherford reads "knocked," "struck." (A reading which, to my eyes, the papyrus text appears to justify as much as the *I*.) Having misread the Greek word for "knocked" or "struck" Rutherford naturally attributes the whole line to one speaker. He reads the third line (and the beginning of line four) like this:

> Someone knocked on the door? who are you? are you
> afraid to come nearer?

He has taken the quick dialogue out of the line, and done so largely on the basis of a variant reading of one word; the reading, *I*, demands the introduction of a second speaker. Whether Rutherford is justified is important; more trained eyes than mine doubt it. But it is even more important, for the present argument, to make it clear again how important a role is played by imaginative intelligence, empathy at work, in the establishment of a text.

One more example will be enough to hold the point. This time the point itself is perhaps less interesting than the previous two; but in this case we have three seriously different interpretations among our three editions, a discrepancy wider than is usually encountered in such comparisons, and one which will illustrate the general problem freshly. It is a question of the seventeenth line of the first mime, whose first part is completely lost in the papyrus. The general thrust of that line, joined to the line following it, will give us something like the following expression, Metriche's words to Gyllis:

> [Oh, stop it] and don't put the blame on time
> [for even though you are old] you are still able,
> Gyllis, to make love.

The three editors fill in both sets of blanks—in lines 17 and 18—differently; and in this case, obviously, they are relying entirely on their sense of what needs to be written there, and their knowledge of what metrical units would be permissible there. In this microscopic case we can say, quite literally, that the editor is forced to recreate the original text. Once again the choices made, which are quite perfunctory, are of less interest than the fact that such

choices are having to be made. All three work with one letter, a
final epsilon: Crusius fits it to *ereide, lean;* Rutherford to *tha-
roune, have courage;* Nairn to *epische, hold on a minute.* Any of
the meanings is possible, none is certain. A similar range of possibilities is exploited at the beginning of the following line.

From these small examples we can only conclude so much
about the kind of scholarship going on among the textual reestab-
lishers of Herondas. Much of what can be concluded has already
become clear; that textual scholarship can never be arid, if the
challenge of it is correctly understood, because that challenge involves a reconstruction of some part of the life of the original text.
It is easy to imagine many poems which would have less of the
creative in them than the good work of textual criticism would
have. (A. E. Housman, by the way, has proved in his edition of
Manilius how fruitfully those two forces of poetry and scholarship
can interact in one life.)

In this light, perhaps, we can see what is being accomplished in
those vast scholarly texts which represent the latest achievements
of Herondas scholarship: in the Headlam-Knox edition (1922), in
Crusius, *Die Mimiamben des Herondas* (1926), in the French
Budé edition (1928) edited and translated by Nairn and Laloy,
and in the latest Italian edition by Puccioni (1950).

When we go back to the original manuscript in its raw state,
with all its problems, we return with a double awareness to these
larger editions: we see that the original has been smothered with
annotation and interpretation; and that for this to have happened
the original must have had tremendous power locked inside it.
(This kind of locking in, encoding of innumerable signified
aspects of a culture, is what we see in its supreme expression in
the Bible, the seeming simplicity of which provides unparalleled
difficulties in interpretation.) The power locked inside Herondas
was in part there simply because our curiosity put it there, com-
mitted us to an intense concern for the cultural world out of
which Herondas made his works. Already in 1891 Rutherford had
expressed the range of the new questions to be awakened and
partially answered by the text of Herondas:

Some books—he wrote—many chapters, very many pages even of
works issued within the year, will have to be rewritten in the light of
the knowledge furnished by the new papyrus. A Curtius or an Osthoff

will have to settle henceforth with the perfects *hororika* and *akēkouka*.
Lexicographers will have to record words either unknown before, or
else existing only in some corrupt passage of an ancient lexicon. Paro-
emiographers will discover that their predecessors knew but a small
number of the proverbs in common use in Greece. The third and the
seventh pieces will add valuable details to books on antiquities. It will
be possible to estimate more accurately the proper place of the mime
in Greek literature.[8]

The lines of questioning, which Rutherford sets out here in the
first excitement of the discovery, are the lines which the major
texts of Herondas pursue. They are in fact the lines we would
expect to find pursued.

Perhaps the most complete of these editions is the massive Knox-
Headlam text; it will be worth concentrating on it briefly, for although the Puccioni text is more recent, and embodies more recent nonliterary information, the Knox-Headlam text resembles it
in many details, and surpasses it in its evident ambition to draw
on every kind of relevant material, and to establish a text, reference to which will from that time on involve reference into the
whole body of the Greek language and its literature. Textual editions like these evidently embody a massive commitment: to re-
experience and bear witness to an ancient author. (Although, for
instance, Puccioni pulls back from many of the Headlam-Knox
conjectures. Puccioni is much more conservative.)

The substance of the Headlam-Knox work is standard: introduction, reestablished texts with notes on variant readings, and
(in this case far the most important) notes on the texts. The notes
are the crown of glory; the triumph of scholarship going beyond
itself. This matter for specialists is throbbing with life. It is hard to
imagine scholarship being given fuller reign than here to draw in
every relevant detail, from modern as well as ancient epigraphy,
numismatics, political history, religious history, literature; or to
imagine scholarship using its privileges with greater humor, discipline, and sense of human relevance. The mark of the most creative scholarship, I suppose, lies precisely here.

The reestablishment of Herondas's text was our main point earlier in this discussion, and it is worth saying that the arguments
flying in the first decade after 1890, those arguments mentioned
earlier, had begun to subside by the second decade of our century.
The text of Knox and Headlam is in most respects fairly definitive

for the present state of affairs; where Crusius and Puccioni differ
it is usually in details of the least importance.

III   *Herondas and Modern Literary-Historical Scholarship*

Scholarship on Herondas has been extensive and we cannot
hope to do more than indicate here some of its chief forms of
creative continuity with its original. There have been in this scholarship, as distinct from the "specifically" textual work on Herondas, certain dominant themes, a few of which I will try to bring
out here. It will be obvious, in bringing them out, that textual and
historical-critical questions are never far apart in matters like this.
(Just as with the Christian Bible, that supreme example, whose
study never grows sophisticated, because it always depends on its
own drawing back to the questions of the connotations of the
Aramaic or Greek words.)

There were, during the first decade of the modern life of Herondas, a great many preliminary scholarly studies, parallel in
topic and ambition to the kind of work that was being done in
establishing the first texts—the kind of work done already in 1891
by Rutherford, by Richard Meister in 1893, by Otto Crusius in
1894, by J. A. Nairn in 1904, and by many other authors—quite a
number of whom published special editions of one mime or another in the learned journals of the day. We can easily get a sense
of this kind of scholarship by pausing over four early and very
detailed instances of it; and over one longer, but even earlier, instance.

The longer piece is Otto Crusius's *Untersuchungen zu den Mimiamben des Herondas* (*Studies of the Mimes of Herondas*),
published in 1892. Each chapter of that book is addressed to a
single mime, the most difficult passages of which are submitted to
careful analysis, some of the most imaginative of which is paro-
emiographic; that is, drawn from Crusius's particular interest in
ancient proverbs and sayings. Crusius is at all times conscious of
the limits of his work; in fact he tells us, in his introduction, about
the agonies of trying to keep up with scholarship in a field in
which scholarship of all kinds is still a necessary basis for any kind
of criticism, and even for basic understanding.

There was no getting around it: the valuable new material had to be
worked through and into again, if the little book was not to come

into the world with "gray hairs." The last chapters stand on an entirely different ground from the first.[9]

Despite this difficulty the book reflects a kind of freshness and critical engagement which are rare; feeling this is realizing how much we miss, in our modern criticism, from lack of exposure to texts in the making. What we do have access to—a single contemporary writer's versions of a single text—invariably strikes us as fresh and illuminating; it acts as a way of loosening up, freeing our sense of the meaning of the final version. This is a different kind of loosening that we get from mulling over the variant versions of an original which have been introduced by the unclarity of a papyrus or by the arguments among editors of texts. But the two kinds of loosening are not so different as they at first appear. In both cases the critic is forced to win back the original from a kind of penumbra of uncertainties, to surround the original and take it by storm. The strategies necessary to this kind of assault engage the critical mind and the critic himself.

The four brief and detailed pieces that I want to consider from this period are taken merely as examples, for already by 1900 there is a bulky literature on Herondas; a bulk which, despite certain underproductive decades, the causes of which would be hard to analyze, a bulk which has grown hugely in the now eighty years since the sands added Herondas to the canon.

The kinds of "perfectly relevant" problems raised here are suggested by a small note in the Dutch periodical *Mnemosyne*: a note written (in Latin) by J. V. Leeuwen in 1897. He wants to propose new ways to read the first words in line 41 (Mime One) and the last words in line 64 (Mime One). Two things are worth discussing here, more than the content of his suggestions. One is that both suggestions were rapidly transcended; later editors, as very often seems to have happened, either ignored or passed on from these suggestions. (If it was a question of "ignoring," which I believe applies in this case, we are forced by the example to reflect both on the extraordinary "wastefulness" of scholarship in the humane sciences, and on a kind of purity, a kind of end-in-itself aspect, to emendations like this one suggested by J. V. Leeuwen.) The other matter is this: we see clearly, in considering such a tiny example, that the difficulties of efforts to establish texts are only exaggerations of the difficulties of criticizing texts.

Two more of these detailed examples can be mentioned, because they amplify the kinds of point just made. Jean Bears in the *Classical Review* (1904) discusses line 96 (Mime Seven) with an eye to a possible reference to Aiolos, the wind-god. That suggestion, I believe, was an inaccurate reading of the papyrus, as well as an unlikely reading. It had, however, a tangential merit; it reached into Hellenistic cultural and religious history, and found its way into an ingenious notion of the significance of Aiolos. There is no room for us to scorn incidental benefits like this, which may in the long run prove to be among scholarship's most fertile growths. Error seems often to be the path to exactitude.

The last example touches one of the first genuinely literary uses to be made of Herondas's texts. It is the article of O. Hense on the second mime of Herondas, which appeared in *Rheinisches Museum* in 1900. The question raised is whether Battaros's speech is like those of the orator Hypereides, one of whose favorite sets of clients was prostitutes. This excellent essay marks a point at which Herondas, having been at least somewhat interpreted and placed in literary history, can be opened out as a writer of great skill, and put not simply into an historical but also into a literary context. The author wins an insight which is in itself not too remarkable, but which is made visible only by scholars' previous efforts to elucidate Herondas:

All in all—he says—one can say that the poet lets his Battaros give off resonances not so much of Hypereides as the whole body of Attic oratory.[10]

With such valid (and well-defended) accounts, Herondas is brought amply into the center of literary studies.

It must be obvious that we can, and will not, treat much of the scholarship on Herondas in this way. There is too much, it is too various, and our conclusions would be much too hard to synthesize. It would be of special interest to form some opinion about the always difficult matter of "progress" in humanistic scholarship. Even without bringing a great deal of the relevant matter to attention here, we will go far enough to support at least some of the conclusions reached in the study of textual scholarship. We will find a preliminary period of fairly pure investigation followed by a period—at which we are arriving in the discussion now—of somewhat freer investigation, itself followed by a certain constricting, a certain turning back toward the original text. It was, unfortunately, hard to make all these points in connection with textual studies, because the issues involved there tended to be highly technical, and hard to expound rapidly. Under other circumstances, however, we would have been able to see much more; in particular some of the many ways in which a first-rate scholar almost of our moment, Puccioni, rejects as fanciful many of the interpretations made by Knox, Headlam, Nairn, and Crusius; and favors the admitting of ignorance in many places where it had seemed abhorrent or unnecessary twenty years before

The cycle I am describing here, and to which I will return more generally later, in looking back over the large matter of the influence of Herondas, reminds us of the constant threat to the "humane sciences," of a weakness in method, or simply of an absence of method. I don't mean the methodology of techniques, of ways to go about handling limited bodies of material: how to address a new papyrus, how to apply archeological or epigraphical data, or how to sort out the dialects intersecting in a literary text. There is by no means a "perfect science" of these matters, which are in any case exceptionally difficult, requiring both patience and imagination. The experts, we find, still make huge blunders in their dating of monuments, deciphering of dedications, or interpreting of fragments: there are in every discipline a great many continuing quarrels over these matters, quarrels attributable to the inevitable differences in human perception, but also to the unusual difficulties presented by ancient Greek culture to the interpreting modern mind. The methodological problem, about which I am thinking here, has to do more generally with the organization of the whole body of classical, as well as of humane, scholarship.

That scholarship has simply grown, as the natural effort of human intelligences, and curiosities, to embrace vast domains of their own preconscious past; it being of great importance in this that scholarship, say classical scholarship, is such an effort at recovery or recuperation. Equally naturally the whole body of that scholarship has grown randomly and casually, without inner direction. The notes and articles considered in the previous pages, and to be mentioned in the following, all responded to the immediate solicitation of a small problem: the problem of what a word meant here, or what kind of influence or resonance was felt there.

We are going to find the same kind of response dominating later writings on Herondas. In a sense this has to be so, both because the period of simply "getting to know" Herondas is still in sway, and because there is much still to get to know. But this lack of guiding direction in the study of Herondas is in miniature a reflection of the same lack in classical studies as a whole, and they of a lack in the humane sciences as a whole. We began on this question by considering, a little prospectively, the stages of Herondas scholarship, which seemed to reflect both random direction and progress in learning. This mixture provides the standard recipe for the study of most classical authors; and constitutes a problem to which we can return, a little better equipped, at the end of this chapter.

A typical enrichment of the study of Herondas's text has been introduced by seeing that literary text in the light of another dimension of experience, say of religious or political. A number of essays raid Herondas for clues to the religion of his world, and in the same act attempt to reflect meaning from that world back onto the texts.

Three characteristic enough examples are the articles by H. J. Rose (*Classical Quarterly,* 1923), W. R. Halliday (*Classical Review,* 1923), and Helen Law (*American Journal of Philology,* 1926); all brief and sharply focused. Rose takes four passages—from mimes one and four—and disputes the Knox-Headlam version of them. (Scholarship on Herondas tends to remain national, to perpetuate national academic traditions. It is always puzzling to find how national modern classical scholarship is, with the exception of a few international efforts, one of which I will soon mention in connection with Herondas: for the most part, the British discuss the British, the Germans the Germans, and so on.) Rose hears resonances of Oriental mystery cults in Herondas's conceptions of the *moirai* and Hekate, which he thinks have escaped Headlam. The corrections he suggests are literary in the sense that they aim to make us better understand the references on the page, and are thus not so far from "textual studies," in general strategy, as we might normally assume. Halliday's article is no more than a note. He discussed the line of Lampriskos (Mime Three, l. 93), addressed to Metriche:

Fie, sirrah! May you find that tongue of yours—dipped in honey.

In Mithraic rites it was customary for the tongue, as well as the hands, to be purified with honey. Though Herondas was probably not close to such cults, Halliday says, superficial knowledge of them was common in Alexandria, and we can assume that Herondas shared that knowledge. Nothing conclusive is possible in such points; they are only conjectures, intending, I suppose, to enrich our reading. It would be hard to say more, or less, than this about either Halliday's or Rose's pieces.

Helen Law's article approaches a religious issue from a more internally literary standpoint. She addresses some simple metaphors in Herondas (Mime Three, l. 92 and Mime Two, ll. 90–91); in the first, Metriche is urging more blows for Kottalos:

Yes, another twenty at least, even if he is going to read better than Klio herself . . . ;

in the second, Battaros says toward the end of his speech:

here, Thales, take me and torture me—only let the damages be placed before the court; not even Minos with his scales could have decided better were he trying us.

For Helen Law this form of hyperbole shows that the poet had no hesitation in declaring mortals superior to gods or heroes. She finds evidence of similar metaphorical clues in other later Greek authors—Theocritos, for example. In this case, I think, her point is at least debatable. It is nearly impossible for us to know how to take metaphors like these. Was Herondas simply using commonplaces? Was he turning a phrase in his own way, and without regard to its theological implications? Or was he, actually, reflecting a changed view of the gods? Helen Law raises these questions, even if she doesn't answer them. And in raising them she finds a fresh angle of attention to Herondas's text.

The three articles just discussed have in common that they try to feel their way into the religious atmosphere of Herondas's world, and into his own mind. It is tempting to say, about groups of articles like this, that in some important way the intelligence they manifest has never been sufficiently taken advantage of. Notes or articles, such as these, have tended to drop into the latency of bibliographies from which they rarely surface. It is hard to know how else this should be. But shouldn't critical editions, at any rate, reflect such patient, though minute, studies? Or, if such studies are *not* worth preserving, should their very claim to publication be challenged at some earlier point in their career? I will return soon to the implications of these questions, which I am so far leaving chiefly rhetorical.

There can in any case be no trouble seeing that the influence of Herondas is being developed, in essays like this; each additional testimony affirms Herondas as a cornerstone of study, and with each such strengthening the impetus toward further scholarship is increased. It is the circle—not vicious, just human—by which cultural canons are affirmed and maintained. It is part of the economics of culture.

Herondas is during this same period entering for the first time into the sphere of a genuinely literary criticism. Examples abound. I will mention only two.

A. Körte, in his *Hellenistic Poetry* (1929), turns a far more sophisticated glance onto Herondas, and the creation of literature, than most people who had preceded him. In discussing the mimes in detail I may have seemed always to be fencing against an unseen opponent, who would claim that Herondas was chiefly, or entirely, noteworthy for his realism. I was in fact attacking a real and persistent tradition of literary scholarship which stopped at the surface of Herondas, making a single valid point but not seeing it in any deeper relationships. Körte breaks with that tradition. For him Herondas is only seemingly "realistic."

There are, to be sure, keenly observed pictures of contemporary life, but they are done in a form that is anything but realistic.[11]

The way he defends this point is lively, and much truer to art than the realistic interpretation. It leads him to a conclusion that the mimes could never had been produced on the stage.

A long essay by M. P. Colombo on the poetry of Herondas appeared in *Dion* in 1934; it touched the finest point reached by literary scholarship on Herondas to that date; perhaps to this date. It is, however, nothing but applied common sense given a literary turn. He sees the modernity of Herondas accurately; his sense of the ugliness of life—a sense which is unsentimental, unlike that of

Theocritos—his ironic pessimism, his deep but not tragic suspicions about human relations. Above all Colombo sees into the bourgeois standpoint from which Herondas works. He manages these perceptions into the distinctive quality of Herondas's "realism," without failing to see Herondas an artist. He is aware that realism of this kind, in order to work, needs also to be artifice.

There is one reason to emphasize the subtlety of this essay; because it is unique in the Herondas scholarship of the period during which it was written. By recognizing this uniqueness we find ourselves discovering, about scholarship on Herondas, what we can find in the scholarship about almost any ancient author, that it is at its weakest in its most purely literary dimensions. This is at first sight a paradoxical discovery, for one is surprised to see that the scholarly study of literature should not regularly, and in some significant sense, also be literary; but this has been the general situation of classical scholarship. With Herondas, to remain with the present example, it will continue to be the situation. The reason for this is not easy to state, though it may be puzzling and worth discussion. To some degree we are here dealing with the problem of the mere difficulty of interpreting, digesting, and communicating classical Greek texts; a difficulty falling far short of that involved with, say, cuneiform texts, but far exceeding that offered by mediaeval French or German tests. But an additional problem seems regularly to have attached itself to this de facto problem. I mean the distance of scholarship from an actual, living handling of texts, as though ancient Greek texts were in effect marked DO NOT HANDLE. That this implication should exist seems improbable enough. But when we read Colombo, and appreciate his subtle, engaged sense of the modernity of Herondas, we understand how much we have been missing in that classical scholarship where literary response to literature is indicated. I am of course excluding from consideration here all those forms of hard scholarship which are in this chapter being viewed as a creative response to Herondas.

The bulk of literary scholarship on Herondas, in this middle period or for that matter at any time, confines itself rather helplessly to repeating the information acquired by scholarship, to retelling plots, and to commenting—far less originally than Colombo or Körte—on Herondas's "realism." This is the case, for ex-

ample, with Émile Cahen's discussion of the mimes which was first
published in 1931, as a supplement to Couat's *Alexandrian Poetry*.
The discussion is brief, but it is typical; and it embodies a dither-
ing which still plagues orthodox literary scholarship.

Of his intention, in writing a few pages on Herondas, he provides a one-sentence description: "Here I shall merely give,"—he
says—"the essential facts and indicate the true character of
Herodes's art" (p. 597). Indicating the true character of this art
means to do several things: it means to give a three- or four-
sentence prose summary of the eight extant mimes; to attempt to
prove that the mimes could not have been performed; and to indicate strongly the sense in which Herondas puts literary art above
"realism." Even the last of these efforts, which is good, is flawed
by a crudely literal conception of that "realism" with which it is
said Herondas became only partly involved. I want to make no
further critique of this kind of literary scholarship than to say that
it contents itself with fairly traditional banalities, which even local
variations cannot finally save. The dilemma of literary scholarship
on Herondas, as on most classical authors, has not at all resulted
from the stupidity of literary scholars, but simply from their real
confusion about what to do with their scholarship. Colombo was
in this respect less confused than Cahen or Körte: which is, in this
case, a way in which Colombo was the most successful of those
men to witness to, and carry farther, the influence of Herondas.

When we come to Herondas scholarship of the last twenty
years we find, naturally enough, that the novelty of the texts has
begun to wear off. The work of digesting Herondas into larger
historical syntheses has gone ahead further; as has the work of
winning an understanding of small details in his work. A brief
glance at those roads of development may at least give us a sense
of direction. It will, I am afraid, give us very little sense of development.

Though nothing is typical in these matters, there is something
representatively small in the article by Lehmann, in the *American
Journal of Archaeology* (1945) on "The Girl Beneath the Apple
Tree." This article concerns a small Hellenistic (or Roman
copied) statuette of a girl who seems to be looking up at the
branches of an apple tree. In lines 27–29 of Mime Four, Kokkale
says to Kynno:

> See, dear, the girl yonder looking up at the apple;
> wouldn't you think she will swoon away suddenly, if
> she does not get it.

The article confines itself to drawing attention to this relationship. What do we gain from such a widening of our field of attention to a passage in Herondas's text?

I have deliberately chosen an example which is small and unpretentious—and not for the first time—because on close, limited inspection we can see the issues more clearly. I believe we want to ask again, when we meet a bearing-forth of Herondas's influence such as this, just what presuppositions it reveals, and what we think of them. Surely one presupposition, of the present small note, is that any roughly contemporary illustrative material, to which we could juxtapose parts of Herondas's text, would help to illuminate or enrich that text; while in the present case the assumption also seems to work in the other direction, suggesting that the text reflects light back onto the art-works. A presumption of mutual enlightenment operates here. What do we think of this presumption, which is of course common enough in scholarship, and in classical scholarship is one of the most familiar forms of bearing witness? Such juxtapositions have an obvious merit; they force us to think about each juxtaposed item freshly; and when the relationship is tangential—even across the arts—and yet piquant, genuinely illustrative, there is the chance that we will see something new, in each of the compared items, which we hadn't seen before. The greatest weakness of such scholarship is that it reflects, in its workings, so little awareness of its own method. As a result, such scholarship plunges ahead, and because the field of possible juxtapositions is infinitely wide and can be run without ground rules, the dangers of indiscriminate juxtaposing are very great. The article by Lehmann is not an example of such lack of discrimination, though it borders on it. It certainly illustrates nearby dangers.

From the small we should go to something larger and synthetic. At the same time we will be reaching toward our own day, and the chronological end of the present discussion of Herondas scholarship.

By larger examples, here, I mean examples drawn from larger works; there are no long works on Herondas alone. The kind of attention he often receives is of the kind we see in Snell's *Poetry and Society* (1961) or Albin Lesky's *History of Greek Literature* (1957–58). Snell's work is a fresh, brief study of the relation between poetry and society in ancient Greek literature. He makes out an extreme but striking case for the newness of Hellenistic poetry. For him Theocritos and Callimachos are the only Greek authors who take no moral stand in their works. They simply paint pictures. Herondas both goes beyond that attitude, in its own direction, and returns from it to an implicitly evaluative standpoint. For Herondas "life is only stupid, rude, and brutal. Even the egotism in which all his characters live has become miserable. Their actions no longer make any sense." [12] Surely this oversimplifies. What about the adulation of Ptolemy? What about the humor? What about the exquisite care for the language itself? What, most important, about the sense of the liveliness of the life portrayed? Snell's thought is often both stimulating and incomplete, as in this statement.

Albin Lesky's massive *History of Greek Literature* contains nothing this controversial. For him the portrayal of the life of society is in Herondas more skillfully reached than it has been before. "His strength lies in the consistently effective use of the realistic components which mark the Hellenistic era," but, he says, "his claim to the title of poet is dubious." [13] Lesky goes on from there to an analysis of the mimes. Those analyses, recountings of "plots," recur almost automatically in studies of Herondas. There is nothing wrong with them; they simply repeat each other, and fail to get far into the texts.

Nothing profound can be made of these words in Snell and Lesky; we cannot hope to see, in them, evidence for the general condition of the most recent Herondas scholarship. There may in fact not be any such general condition. There have been no recent books devoted to Herondas. What has been written has tended either to address details, like a number of articles I have discussed, or to encase Herondas in the large words of a large work like Lesky's. At the end of my discussion of textual studies of Herondas I was able to point to the most recent text, Puccioni's; and to remark how much more conservative it was than the Headlam-Knox text. It seemed as though a new Protestantism, a hypercareful return to the sources, had set in with the sixties. I think it would be impossible even to make such a timid generalization concerning scholarship—textual scholarship—on Herondas. It is what it is. It has no marked direction, or avant-garde, at this point. There is nothing inherently bad in this state of affairs. But it is worth realizing that this need *not* be the state of affairs; there are alternative situations, as we could imagine, given the essential freedom behind the human desire to maintain the creative tradition of scholarship about a man's works.

One alternative would be a more concerted sociological attention to Herondas's work. It is, as Snell says, remarkable about Herondas that he portrays society so that it *feels real;* we believe we are touching his society, through the traits of it he offers us. In my analysis of the mimes I stressed the artifice with which Herondas manages this realism; and I would, in fact, not care to dissolve the discussion of Herondas into amateur literary sociology. But a "sociologically" grounded analysis of him, which looked out always from the viewpoint of literature, would have something to add. That something would not be only what we find in Carl Schneider's massive *Kulturgeschichte des Hellenismus;* in which material facts are plundered, from all kinds of literary works, in order to build up a description of the "world" (the *Lebenswelt*) of a period. The sociological analysis of which I am thinking would be able to embody great respect for the aesthetic element in literature, as we see occurring in the work of Theodor Adorno.

IV *Herondas and Translations*

Translators of Herondas make up my last category of bearing witness to his living influence. In turning to this matter we are not leaving behind the matters of textual tradition and pure scholarship, which we took up earlier. (Nor in considering those activities were we far from the kinds of question posed by the good translator to himself, about the work he is translating.) It will therefore be explicit enough, if we touch on a very few samples, from the large body of Herondas translations already in existence.

The first translator I want to touch is John Addington Symonds, who anticipates the point I have just finished making:

I am, therefore, well aware that no translation of Herondas at the present time can aspire to literary quality, and that the best will be found full of blunders when the microscropical analysis of several generations shall have wrought agreement upon all the numerous disputed passages.[14]

The translations which he offers, of the mimes extant at this time, are in prose and, as we would expect, felicitous and flowing, with all the lacunae filled in. We can make our point by comparing a particular passage in Symonds' translation to those of Headlam and Knox, and Lindsay; the two other specimens. A look at the opening lines of the fifth mime will bring out the differences in style and verbal strategy among these three translations into English. It will also give us some idea of the kinds of testimony which translation can be to the living force of an author.

Symonds begins with:

Bitinna: Tell me, Gastron, you, sir! are you grown so dainty that I cannot content you, but you must needs be running after Menon's Amphytaea?

Gastron: I after Amphytaea! Did I ever see the woman you are talking of?

Bitinna: You're always putting me off with excuses.

Gastron: Bitinna, I am a slave; so do what you like with me. But don't go on sucking my blood night and day.[15]

Though all these translations pretty up Bitinna's first speech, Symonds does it most; substituting "running after" for "having intercourse with." But his literary sense is fine; though he is the least "academic" of the English translators of Herondas, he is in an important sense the most accurate. His feeling for the dramatic interplay, between mistress and slave, is living and complete, and gives us back the instigation to get into Herondas's world again. It is hard to distinguish the final intention of work like this from that of good scholarship and textual criticism.

We have already paid some attention to the Headlam-Knox translation, which was in fact made in the closest possible relation to establishing Herondas's text and annotating it. For the section in question they give us:

Bitinna: Tell me, Gastron, have you waxed so fat, that my legs are not enough for your sport, but you must press your suit with Amphytaea, wife of Menon.

Gastron: I! Amphytaea! Have I ever seen this woman you are talking of?

Bitinna: Every day excuses and excuses!

Gastron: Bitinna, I am your slave; do what you will with me, and don't suck my blood every day and every night.[16]

"Press your suit," in Bitinna's first speech, is the expected concession to the British language of that day, and in that general concession this translation resembles the work of Symonds. But the resemblance between the two translations, in this passage and throughout, is surprisingly great. One finds in both Symonds and Headlam-Knox a kind of translation-language. It is prosaic—paying, in the present case, no attention to the careful choliambic strategy of Herondas. It relies greatly on a generalized form of the diction of English fiction—that, for example, of Hardy or Eliot; a diction not in fact drawn from the common speech of men, but from a literary version of that common speech. I felt, in trying to put forth Herondas into this book, that the Headlam-Knox translation was the best available: for reasons inherent to it, and because in its way it touched something of that literary archaizing, combined with fairly gritty speech, which characterized Herondas's language. It is quite possible that a writer like Samuel Butler —if fate had allowed—might have been the perfect translator of Herondas. *Hudibras* is written in a style which might have caught even Herondas's style.

My third example is the most recent, from Jack Lindsay; translations included in his *Ribaldry of Ancient Greece* (1961). He begins this way:

Bitinna: So, Gastron, you're so bored with me you slight the freedom of my body that I gave you, and pluck at Menon's wife, that Amphytaia.

Gastron: What, her? I've never even seen the woman you mention.

Bitinna: Every day a fresh excuse.

Gastron: Bitinna, I'm your slave, I do your will, but please don't suck my blood all day and night.[17]

Lindsay preserves a formal version of Herondas's verse form, and in spirit tends to break with the prosaic. But his language, in translating Herondas, is far even from the vigor of that (slightly unreal) diction achieved by Symonds and Headlam-Knox. "Pluck at," in Bitinna's first speech, illustrates the point well enough.

There is no reason, here, to say more about the relation of translation to the other forms of scholarship discussed in this chapter. And there is very little excuse for a generalization about the development of the tradition of translating Herondas. Perhaps one point needs stressing, for what it is worth: much of the early translation of, as well as the early scholarship on, Herondas was among the best work done in relation to Herondas. I believe that something of this sort would turn out to be true about the scholarly work devoted to a number of ancient Greek poets.

V *The General Character of the Modern Testimony to Herondas*

This chapter has concerned the influence of Herondas, influence in a broadly understood sense. We began by pointing out the complexity of what we call the creative process, and some of the difficulties involved in the orthodox distinctions between scholarship and creative work. Fresher distinctions opened the way to a fresher view of the still short tradition of scholarship on Herondas. That tradition has existed for only a short time; yet we can already see at least nascent patterns in it.

My main attention here has been directed to the witness borne to Herondas as a new member of the literary community. A much more general problem has been in the background all the time; the problem of the grounding of scholarship about ancient literature; and, with no extravagant extension, the grounding of literary scholarship in general. By viewing scholarship as creativity I gave some indication of my view of one solution to this problem. In many senses, however, scholarship is *not* poetry, but has tendencies and methodological emphases that set it apart.

The problem of Herondas scholarship is illustrative. Basic work had to be done toward establishing the text and the fundamental meanings of this new author. He had to be put in a cultural and political-historical context. He had to be literally interpreted, up to a certain point. He had to be translated. Only after much of this work had been done did the question begin to raise itself; what kind of cognitive inquiry is underway here? This late but sharp intrusion of methodological concern has often broken into the peace of classical scholarship, and literary scholarship in general.

How can we elaborate the question of methodology in the very limited case of Herondas? What are we trying to do by studying him as we do? Is there any other way to study him? We can conclude this chapter by taking up these questions, not so much in order as in their unity, in the demand which they come together to assert.

One feels that, in the case of the study of Herondas, there is too much random activity. I hope that by going into several small and detailed aspects of Herondas scholarship, I have given some sense of this randomness. I have of course touched only on a few isolated instances, while pointing out that the bibliography of works, on Herondas alone, is already huge. But what has been discussed, the little that was noted here, has hardly been digested into the small body even of Herondas scholarship.

To say this, however, is to imply that the problem in the method of studying Herondas is essentially one of collating the studies made, and of making them widely, internationally, available. This in itself is no small problem; the solution of it would require a good deal of preliminary work, which would at one extreme be purely mechanical, and at the other extreme would require a high degree of perception into the whole scholarly process, a broad vision of that process. Clearly something like that solution would be very desirable, and within our power. A computer filled with the basic information, contained in studies of Herondas, would be a quite sufficient, and thoroughly efficient, source of knowledge of what has been done.

A deeper question is raised in considering the studies devoted to Herondas. Are those studies close enough to their object, or do they too quantify and lose it? I have wanted to show, throughout this chapter, the closeness of scholarship to creativity. What I suggest now is not a different point, but it bears a different emphasis. Even while exercising its inner creativity, as we have seen it doing in textual studies, scholarship and translation, even in exercising creativity in those dimensions, scholarship as we see it here runs a serious danger of being about itself, of being only self-referential, rather than being about a figure of the Hellenic past.

What, then, is the creativity I am attributing to scholarship, if it is not a going-close to its object, a feeling its way into the object? It is at its best nothing but that; it is a living testimony. However, it needs to be an organized testimony in order to be as effective as it can inherently be. I think we can return, on this note, to the question of order and organization in scholarship.

Something can be achieved toward that order and organization by the development of mechanisms for unity; computers, international information-pools, volumes of synthesis, and others. However, for such order as that to be meaningful, there needs to be more order near the ground of production of scholarship, no matter how creative and empathetic scholarship may be. I mean that there needs to be more inherent and spontaneous unity to the productions of that scholarship. But a paradox is lodged here.

There needs to be more inherent unity in classical scholarship. In studies of Herondas there need to be more generally agreed on, and felt, priorities. By such priorities I mean, for example: the desirability of understanding the whole work of Herondas in its cultural context; of understanding the whole contribution of the Greek language, in its dialectic forms, to the language of Herondas; of understanding the total heritage from Herondas. The whole in every case establishes the priority. (I think here not only of the study of Herondas, or of Greek literature, but of ancient culture as a whole.) There is an important sense in which the whole, in such matters, is prior to its parts, for only the cultural whole gives meaning to the cultural parts. But now we are close to the paradox.

The sense of priorities, which I am indicating schematically here, cannot be imposed, or made part of a "platform" for scholarship. This sense needs to grow from the roots of a culture. The cultural roots from which our classical—and Herondaean—scholarship has grown have produced valuable and creative work of the kind discussed in this chapter. But that work has little inherent unity. If we value such unity, and would like to see it there, we must change, as we optimistically put it, the appropriate areas of our culture.

Herondas scholarship is no area in which to begin the revolution, to begin any revolution. Perhaps I have said, in the preface to this book, all that is appropriate in the present context; that we must try to take Herondas on us personally, at the point where we are immediately, therefore generally, human. To do this would mean that each of us would go beyond himself, as far as was congruent with his own gifts, into that fund of general humanity each of us is and draws from. The real unity of scholarship on Herondas would rise from there.

Notes and References

Preface

1. For an account of this discovery, convenient reference can be made to the Headlam and Knox edition of *Herodas: The Mimes and Fragments* (Cambridge, 1922). I draw freely on the work of Headlam and Knox.

2. For studies of such text histories the standard general work is still J. E. Sandys, *A History of Classical Scholarship* (new printing; New York, 1967.

3. The necessary book on the formation of the classical literary canon still needs to be written. It would draw together the resources of classical scholarship with those of contemporary sociology of knowledge. We still need to refer to books like Gilbert Highet's *The Classical Tradition* (New York, 1949) or E. M. Butler's *The Tyranny of Greece over Germany* (Boston, 1958).

4. The second part of that book—"Elements of Semiology"—is a convenient survey of this linguistic position, whose chief inspiration was the work of the French linguist, De Saussure.

Chapter One

1. For many of these points I rely on two works: A. B. Burn, *The Lyric Age of Greece* (London, 1960), and Max Treu, *Von Homer zur Lyrik* (*From Homer to the Lyric*) (Munich, 1955).

2. For the general traits of the Homeric world cf. M. I. Finley, *The World of Odysseus* (New York, 1954). On the "moral world" of Homer, see A. W. Adkins, *Merit and Responsibility* (Oxford, 1960).

3. W. W. Tarn, *Hellenistic Civilization* (London, 1930), p. 4. Tarn's book is a good guide to the culture of a period which has by now been overwhelmed by scholarly comment.

4. Hermann Reich, *Der Mimus* (Berlin, 1903), provides a comprehensive and detailed history of the mime in antiquity.

Chapter Two

1. Giulio Puccioni, *Herondas: Mimiambi* (Florence, 1950), p. lx.

2. *Ibid.*, p. ix.

3. Headlam and Knox, *Herodas*, p. lxi.

4. *Ibid.*, p. xxix.

5. There is a huge literature on the "literary type," on that aspect of the general in literature. A useful summary of the issues can be found in Wellek and Warren, *The Theory of Literature* (New York, 1942), pp. 226–29.

6. It is worth mentioning two recent texts which bring large areas of this thought into the clear: Lemon and Reis, *Russian Formalist Criticism* (Lincoln, 1965) and *Qu'est-ce que le Structuralisme* (Paris, 1968), edited by several hands.

7. I have to pass brusquely over the very delicate question of how the literary text reflects neurosis. That reflection cannot be direct, and it is always mediated through the artifice in art. The classic study, of the entire relation of the creator's experience to his work, is still Wilhelm Dilthey's *Das Erlebnis und die Dichtung* (*Experience and Poetry*) (Leipzig, 1912).

8. Tzvetan Todorov, *Grammaire du Décaméron* (Paris, 1969).

9. It is, I know, unusual to use these mood-terms in literary historical discussion. To justify their use, at all thoroughly, I would have to begin with an analysis of Otto Bollnow's seminal *Das Wesen der Stimmungen* (*The Being of Moods*) (Frankfurt, 1943).

10. Walzel's works, like *Gehalt und Gestalt im dichterischen Kunstwerk* (*Content and Form in the Literary Art-Work*) have much to offer to the student, of the inside of works, who wants to preserve a language of rational communication while talking about the inner character of art.

11. Headlam and Knox, *Herodas*, p. i of Introduction.

Chapter Three

1. Carl Schneider's recent *Kulturgeschichte des Hellenismus* (*Cultural History of Hellenism*) (Munich, 1967) gives a copious documentation to these matters. There is no better place to establish our sense of the material realities of Hellenistic culture.

2. Many aspects of this situation in the ancient world are well suggested in G. C. Fiske, *Lucilius and Horace* (Madison, 1920).

3. I have treated this question at more length in an essay, "Publica Materies," *Arion*, II (1963) 131–42.

4. Georg Kaibel, *Comicorum Graecorum Fragmenta* (Berlin, 1899). Fragments 1, 3, 6 of Sophron.

5. Headlam and Knox, *Herodas*, p. xxiv.

Chapter Four

1. Pliny the Younger, IV, iii, 14–18.

2. These fragmentary mimes are collected in the back (pp. 402–17) of Headlam and Knox, *Herodas.*

3. Quoted by Headlam and Knox, *Herodas,* p. 421.

4. Pliny the Younger, VI, 21, 4.

5. Cited by Headlam and Knox, *Herodas,* p. 410.

6. Cited by Crusius, *Untersuchungen zu den Mimiamben des Herondas* (*Studies of the Mimes of Herondas*), p. iv.

7. Sir Frederic Kenyon, *Classical Texts* (London, 1891) p. 6.

8. W. G. Rutherford, *Herondas* (London, 1907), pp. vii-viii.

9. Crusius, *Untersuchungen,* p. iv.

10. O. Hense, "Zum II. Mimiamb des Herondas" ("On the Second Mime of Herondas"), *Rheinisches Museum,* 55 (1900), 222–31.

11. Alfred Körte, *Hellenistic Poetry* (Leipzig, 1925), p. 327.

12. Bruno Snell, *Poetry and Society* (Bloomington, 1961), p. 109.

13. Albin Lesky, *History of Greek Literature* (Bern, 1957–58), p. 748.

14. J. A. Symonds, *Studies of the Greek Poets* Vol. II (New York, 1880), p. 243.

15. *Ibid.,* p. 253.

16. Headlam and Knox, *Herodas,* p. 221.

17. Jack Lindsay, *The Ribaldry of Ancient Greece* (New York, 1965), p. 139.

Selected Bibliography

(I include works which have been of particular value to me, and in most cases attach a few descriptive or critical words.)

PRIMARY SOURCES

1. Texts

CRUSIUS, OTTO. *Die Mimiamben des Herondas.* Leipzig: Dieterich, 1926. Excellent literary annotations.

HEADLAM, WALTER and KNOX, A. D., *Herodas: The Mimes and Fragments.* Cambridge: Cambridge University Press, 1922. The main scholarly support of my arguments in this book.

NAIRN, J. A. and LALOY, L. *Les Mimes.* Paris: Les Belles Lettres, 1960.

PUCCIONI, GIULIO. *Herondas: Mimiambi.* Florence: La Nuova Italia, 1950. The most recent edition of Herondas.

2. Translations

CRUSIUS, OTTO. *Die Mimiamben des Herondas.* Leipzig: Dieterich, 1926. Excellent colloquial feeling for the originals.

KNOX, A. D. In *Herodas: The Mimes and Fragments.* Cambridge: Cambridge University Press, 1922. The versions I have used in this book. Semi-archaic English managed with understanding.

LALOY, LOUIS. In *Les Mimes.* Paris: Les Belles Lettres, 1960.

PUCCIONI, GIULIO. In his *Herondas: Mimiambi.* Florence: La Nuova Italia, 1950.

SYMONDS, J. A. In his *Studies of the Greek Poets.* Vol. II. New York: Harper and Brothers, 1880. Good but dated.

SECONDARY SOURCES

1. Books

ADLER, ALFRED. *Understanding Human Nature.* New York: Greenberg, 1927. A psychological classic on the theory of human character-types.

KÖRTE, ALFRED. *Hellenistic Poetry.* Leipzig: Kroner, 1925. A good
general survey of the literary world in which Herondas worked.

CRUSIUS, OTTO. *Untersuchungen zu den Mimiamben des Herondas*
(*Studies of the Mimes of Herondas*). Leipzig: Teubner, 1892.

LANGER, SUZANNE, *Mind; An Essay on Human Feelings.* Baltimore;
Johns Hopkins Press, 1967. Takes up the psychology of crea-
tive experience in such a way that it bears on this study of
Herondas.

LESKY, ALBIN. *Geschichte der griechischen Literatur* (*History of
Greek Literature*). Bern: Francke, 1957–58. A massive study
of Greek literature.

REICH, HERMANN. *Der Mimus.* Berlin: Weidmann, 1903. The most
comprehensive treatment of the literary subgenre in which
Herondas wrote.

RUTHERFORD, W. G. *Herondas.* London: Macmillan, 1907. A chal-
lenging if often mistaken early edition and analysis of the poet.

SCHNEIDER, CARL. *Kulturgeschichte des Hellenismus.* Munich: Beck,
1967. My chief reference point for the material culture of the
Hellenistic world.

SNELL, BRUNO. *Poetry and Society.* Bloomington, 1961.

TARN, W. W. *Hellenistic Civilization.* London: Arnold, 1930. A
classic.

2. Articles

BEARE, JOHN. "Herondas VIII: 96," *Classical Review,* 18 (1904),
287–88. Exemplary close study of a single variant reading.

COLOMBO, M. P. "La poesia di Eronda," *Dion,* IV (1934), 100–119.
One of the best existing literary studies of Herondas.

CRUSIUS, OTTO and HERZOG, RUDOLF. "Der Traum des Herondas"
("The Dream of Herondas"), *Philologus,* 79 (1924), 370–433.
Fine example of an exhaustive study of one Mime, here the
eighth.

EDMONDS, J. M. "Some Notes on the Herondas Papyrus," *Classical
Quarterly,* 19 (1925), 129–46. Example of a thorough papyro-
logical study.

HALLIDAY, W. R. "Herondas. Mime III, 93," *Classical Review,* 36–37
(1923), 115 ff. Uses religious history effectively to elucidate
a text.

HERZOG, RUDOLF. "Herondas," *Philologus,* 82 (1927), 27–66. Close
study of the situation of Herondas scholarship, at date of
article. A landmark in survey of the nature and limits of such
scholarship.

KNOX, A. D. "The Dream of Herodas," *Classical Review,* 38 (1925),
13–15. Particularly interesting as a sample from a long, intellec-

tually lively, controversy between Knox and Herzog over the interpretation of Herondas.

LAW, HELEN. "Hyperbole in Mythological Comparisons," *American Journal of Philology*, 47 (1926), 361–72. Analysis of some metaphors in Herondas.

LEHMANN-HARTLEBEN, K. "The Girl Beneath the Apple-Tree," *American Journal of Philology*, 47 (1945), 430–33. Example of thinking by drawing an analogy between visual and literary art.

PACE, B. "Mimo e attor mimico," *Dion* III (1931), 162–72. Discusses the continuing popular tradition of the mime, since antiquity, in Sicily and South Italy.

ROSE, H. J. "Quaestiones Herondeae," *Classical Quarterly*, 7 (1923), 32–34. Questioning of Headlam-Knox edition on many points, most of them connected with religious history.

Index

145

DATE DUE

GAYLORD			PRINTED IN U.S.A.